Oxford International English

3

Myra Murby

OXFORD
UNIVERSITY PRESS

OXFORD
UNIVERSITY PRESS

Great Clarendon Street, Oxford OX2 6DP

Oxford University Press is a department of the University of Oxford.
It furthers the University's objective of excellence in research, scholarship,
and education by publishing worldwide in

Oxford New York

Auckland Cape Town Dar es Salaam Hong Kong Karachi
Kuala Lumpur Madrid Melbourne Mexico City Nairobi
New Delhi Shanghai Taipei Toronto

With offices in

Argentina Austria Brazil Chile Czech Republic France Greece
Guatemala Hungary Italy Japan Poland Portugal Singapore
South Korea Switzerland Thailand Turkey Ukraine Vietnam

© Oxford University Press 2013

British Library Cataloguing in Publication Data

Data available

ISBN- 978-019839031-2

10 9 8 7 6 5 4 3 2

Printed in Malaysia by Vivar Printing Sdn. Bhd.

Paper used in the production of this book is a natural, recyclable product made from wood
grown in sustainable forests. The manufacturing process conforms to the environmental
regulations of the country of origin.

Acknowledgements

The author and publisher are grateful for permission to reprint the following copyright
material:

Jill Atkins: *Yasmin's Parcels* (Readzone, 2013), copyright © Jill Atkins 2008, reprinted by
permission of Readzone Books Ltd and the author.

Neil Buchanan: 'Magic Mask' from *Great Art Attack Stuff* (DK, 1999), copyright © Dorling
Kindersley Ltd 1999, reprinted by permission of Dorling Kindersley Ltd.

Lauren Child: extracts from *Utterly Me, Clarice Bean* (Orchard Books, 2003), copyright © Lauren
Child 2003, reprinted by permission of David Higham Associates.

Roald Dahl: letter to his mother, original kept at the Roald Dahl Museum and Story Centre,
reprinted by permission of Dahl and Dahl Ltd.

John Foster: 'The Young Fox' from *Senses Poems chosen by John Foster* (OUP, 1996, 2005), copyright
© John Foster 1996, reprinted by permission of the author.

Janine M Fraser: *Abdullah's Butterfly* illustrated by Kim Gamble (Collins, 1998), text copyright ©
Janine M Fraser 1997, reprinted by permission of HarperCollins Publishers, Australia

Janet Grierson: extract from *Maui Catches the Sun* (Edgy Productions, 2006), reprinted by
permission of Edgy Productions Ltd .

Roger McGough: 'The Sound Collector' from *Pillow Talk* (Viking, 1990), copyright © Roger
McGough 1990, reprinted by permission of Peters Fraser & Dunlop (www.petersfraserdunlop.
com) on behalf of the author.

John Malam: 'Desert Meerkats' from *Going Underground* (Project X, OUP, 2009), copyright ©
Oxford University Press 2009, reprinted by permission of Oxford University Press.

Alexander McCall Smith: extracts from *Precious and the Monkeys* (Polygon, 2011), published in
the USA as *The Great Cake Mystery* (Random House, 2011), copyright © Alexander McCall Smith
2011, reprinted by permission of David Higham Associates, and Random House Inc.

UNICEF: 'Michael', from *A Life Like Mine: How children live around the world* (DK in association with
UNICEF, 2002, 2006), copyright © Dorling Kindersley Ltd 2002, reprinted by permission of
Dorling Kindersley Ltd.

Gini Wade: extracts from *Kesuna and the Cave Demons, Folk Tales of the World: A Balinese Folk Tale*
(Dutton Children's Books, 1995), copyright © Gini Wade 1995, reprinted by permission of
Penguin Books Ltd.

Kit Wright: 'Dad and the Cat and the Tree' from *The Magic Box* (Macmillan Children's Books,
2009), copyright © Kit Wright 1999, reprinted by permission of the author.

Any third party use of this material, outside of this publication, is prohibited. Interested
parties should apply to the copyright holders indicated in each case.

Although we have made every effort to trace and contact all copyright holders before
publication this has not been possible in all cases. If notified, the publisher will rectify any
errors or omissions at the earliest opportunity.

The publisher and authors would like to thank the following for permission to use
photographs and copyright material.

p8: titov dmitriy/Shutterstock; p8l (inset): © Werli Francois/Alamy; p8r (inset): © Tim Gainey/
Alamy; p9: © View Stock/Alamy; p12: col/Shutterstock; p13: suns07/Shutterstock; p16: Kozoriz
Yuriy/Shutterstock; p24: Vladimir Gerasimov/Shutterstock; p24 (inset): Robert Adrian Hillman/
Shutterstock; p25: © Ocean/Corbis; p29t: Steve Collender/Shutterstock; p29c: suvijakra/
Shutterstock; p29b: Poznyakov/Shutterstock; p32: Bjorn Stefanson/Shutterstock; p33: © James
Davies/Alamy; p34: Bjorn Stefanson/Shutterstock; p36t: Dragan Milovanovic/Shutterstock; p37t:
USBFCO/Shutterstock; p37b: © Inspirestock/Corbis; p38: margouillat photo/Shutterstock; p39:
kickstand/iStockphoto; p40: zahradales/Shutterstock; p40 (inset): © James Hardy/PhotoAlto/
Corbis; p41t: Valentina Razumova/Shutterstock; p41cr: mkm3/Shutterstock; p41cl: Evgeny
Karandaev/Shutterstock; p41b: © Plush Studios/Blend Images/Corbis; p45t: Menno Schaefer/
Shutterstock; p49t: Matthew Williams-Ellis/Shutterstock; p54: izarizhar/Shutterstock; p54l:
kerriekerr/iStockphoto; p54r: © Blaine Harrington III/Alamy; p55tr: ermess/Shutterstock; p55b:
Ellerslie/Shutterstock; p59: Jason Ho/Shutterstock; p62: nopporn/Shutterstock; p62b:
Lightspring/Shutterstock; p65: Brian Kinney/Shutterstock; p67t: abimages/Shutterstock; p70:
Zurbagan/Shutterstock; p70 (inset): Getty/Don Boroughs; p71: Yuriy Boyko/Shutterstock; p71b:
© T.M.O.Pictures/Alamy; p80: Markus Mainka/Shutterstock; p82: rodho/Shutterstock; p83t:
mhatzapa/Shutterstock; p86: Tupungato/Shutterstock; p86 (inset): © Amy Toensing/National
Geographic Society/Corbis; p87: Ruth Black/Shutterstock; p91t: © Frans Lanting/Corbis; p96:
Monkey Business Images/Shutterstock; p97l: Stargazer/Shutterstock; p101b: Bruce Rolff/
Shutterstock; p101t: Undergroundarts.co.uk/Shutterstock; p104: Jamen Percy/Shutterstock;
p108: Lars Christensen/Shutterstock; p109t: Aleksandr Bryliaev/Shutterstock; p109b: Denis
Semenchenko/Shutterstock; p110: Ivonne Wierink/Shutterstock; p113: ecco/Shutterstock; p116:
Karen Gentry/Shutterstock; p116r: © imagebroker/Alamy; p118r: © Bill Bachman/Alamy; p119:
© Bill Bachman/Alamy; p120l: amygdala_imagery/iStockphoto; p120r: kwest/Shutterstock;
p122: AnetaPics/Shutterstock; p123: Pichugin Dmitry/Shutterstock; p127: Daniel Alvarez/
Shutterstock; p128: Denise Thompson/Shutterstock; p129: Eric Isselee/Shutterstock; p132tl:
Hugh Lansdown/Shutterstock; p132tr: © blickwinkel/Alamy; p13b: © Juniors Bildarchiv GmbH/
Alamy; p133: Richard Susanto; p136: Dmitry Kovtun/Shutterstock.

Background Images: p1images/iStockphoto; Sergej Razvodovskij/Shutterstock; Thampapon/
Shutterstock; ecco/Shutterstock.

Cover illustration: Fernando Juarez

Artwork is by: Akbar Ali, Gaynor Barrs; Mark Beech; Beccy Blake; Patricia Castelao; Alex
Colombo; James Cottell; Pippa Curnick; Emil Dacanay; Paolo Domeniconi; John Kelly; Richard
Morgan; Martin Remphrey; Emma Shaw-Smith; Kristina Swarner; Katri Valkamo.

Contents

A world of stories, poems and facts 4

Unit contents 6

1 **Home and school** 8

2 **Find out how!** 24

3 **Our sensational senses** 40

Revise and check 1 52

4 **Traditional tales** 54

5 **Keep in touch!** 70

6 **Sharing cultures** 86

Revise and check 2 98

7 **It's a mystery!** 100

8 **Our world** 116

9 **Why do we laugh?** 132

Revise and check 3 144

Reading fiction
Yasmin's Parcels 146

A world of stories, poems and facts

ALASKA

NORTH AMERICA

UK

EUROPE

ATLANTIC OCEAN

PACIFIC OCEAN

SOUTH AMERICA

ARCTIC OCEAN

ASIA

AFRICA

Gir Forest

MALAYSIA

BALI

INDIAN OCEAN

OTSWANA

Kalahari Desert

AUSTRALIA

NEW ZEALAND

OCEANIA

SOUTHERN OCEAN

ANTARCTICA

Unit contents

Unit	Theme	Reading and comprehension
1	Home and school	**Fiction** Narrative with a familiar setting *Abdullah's Butterfly*
2	Find out how!	**Non-fiction** Instructions *How to Make a Mask, How to Make a Grass Head*
3	Our sensational senses	**Poems** Poetry about the senses, *The Sound Collector, The Young Fox*
	REVISE AND CHECK UNITS 1–3	
4	Traditional tales	**Fiction** Traditional narrative *A Balinese Folk Tale*
5	Keep in touch!	**Non-fiction** *Letter to author from Clarice Bean, Letter from author to Clarice and Betty, Letter from Roald Dahl to his mother*
6	Sharing cultures	**Play script** A play based on a Maori legend *Maui Catches the Sun*
	REVISE AND CHECK UNITS 4–6	
7	It's a mystery!	**Fiction** Mystery narrative *Precious and the Monkeys*
8	Our world	**Non-fiction** Non-chronological reports, *Michael, Desert Meerkats*
9	Why do we laugh?	**Poem** Humorous narrative poem *Dad and the Cat and the Tree*
	REVISE AND CHECK UNITS 7–9	
	FICTION READING *Yasmin's Parcels*	

Language, grammar, spelling, vocabulary, phonics, punctuation	Writing	Speaking and listening
• Unfamiliar words, definitions • Nouns, adjectives and verbs • Powerful verbs and adjectives • New spellings, syllables and vowels • Features of fiction genre	Fiction Writing a story with a familiar setting	Organization of ideas Language choices Confident talking in turns
• New words in context • Instructions vocabulary • Sentences • Imperative verbs • Question marks and exclamation marks • Tenses, present and past • Spelling, adding -ed and -ing to verbs • Features of instruction text	Non-fiction Writing a set of instructions	Expressing opinions Instructions – listening and understanding
• Unfamiliar words, definitions • Senses vocabulary • Prefixes, un-, dis-, re-, pre- and de- • Features of poetry genre	Play script Writing a play script	Language choices Confident talking in discussion Poetry performance
• New words in context • Synonyms • Thesaurus and extension of vocabulary • Alternative words for 'said' • Speech punctuation • Features of traditional tales and legends	Fiction Rewriting a traditional story	Questions – develop ideas and extend understanding Language choices
• Unfamiliar words, definitions • Letters vocabulary • Suffixes, -ful, -less, -ly • Singular and plural • Apostrophes in contractions • Features of letters	Non-fiction Writing a formal letter	Expressing opinions Organization of ideas
• New words in context • Irregular verbs, 'to be' • Alphabetical ordering • Dictionaries • Features of play scripts • Features of poetry genre	Poetry Writing a poem	Language choices Poetry performance Listening and confident talking in turns
• Unfamiliar words, definitions • Prefixes, non-, mis-, anti-, co- and ex- • Pronouns • Singular and plural • Agreement of verbs • Features of fiction genre	Fiction Writing an adventure story	Expressing opinions Organization of ideas
• New words in context • Irregular verbs, 'to have', 'to go' • Compound words • Compound sentences and connectives • Complex sentences and commas • Features of non-chronological reports	Non-fiction Writing a non-chronological report	Expressing opinions Questions – ideas and understanding
• Unfamiliar words, definitions • Dictionary, thesaurus and extension of vocabulary • Homonyms • Rhyme • Features of poetry genre	Poetry Writing a limerick	Poetry performance Language choices

1 Home and school

Let's Talk

1 Look at these pictures. What do you think is happening?

2 Where is your home and how do you get to school in the morning? Do you walk, travel by bus or go in a car?

"He who asks a question is a fool for a minute; he who does not remains a fool forever."

Chinese proverb

Describing journeys to school

 Read the words in the Word Cloud and match them to the meanings here.

1 A person who rides a bicycle.

2 A person who is walking along the road.

3 A trip from one place to another.

Word Cloud
cyclist
journey
pedestrian

 Rewrite the sentences below and use the following words to fill the gaps.

catch   bus   late

Each morning, the school _bus_ stops in my village.

I am often _late_ and have to run to _catch_ it!

 Work with a partner and describe your journey to school. How are your journeys similar and how are they different?

9

Stories with familiar settings

This story is about a boy called Abdullah, who lives in a mountain village in Malaysia. Abdullah catches butterflies and sells them to a local craft shop. He uses the money to buy special porridge for his grandfather.

Abdullah's Morning

Each day, as Abdullah sets off for school he shrugs into the straps of his satchel and snatches up his butterfly net from beside the door. His mother puts in papaya and
5 banana and flat pancakes for his lunch. She smooths his hair and tells him to study hard and listen to the teacher, because she wants him to do better than weave baskets and catch butterflies for the rest of his life.

10   But Grandfather reaches for his hand as he is going out the door and whispers in his ear.

"Catch me a butterfly today Abdullah, a big green butterfly if you can."

And Abdullah knows that Grandfather is
15 hungry for the porridge that he likes so much because his teeth are all gone.

...Abdullah rode down early to the town as usual, in the rattly old yellow school bus with the tall black writing on its side. SEKOLAH,
20 it says. School.

...As the bus bumped and swerved down the mountain, Abdullah kept watch out of the window, twirling his net gently in his hands, hoping to be lucky enough to see a large,
25 bright butterfly.

...Abdullah studied hard, as his mother told him. He studied maths and English and faraway countries. He wrote carefully in his book and listened to Mr Ginyun, but all the
30 while he kept one eye watching out the window for a butterfly for Grandfather.

From *Abdullah's Butterfly* by Janine M. Fraser and Kim Gamble

Glossary

butterfly
an insect with four brightly coloured wings

porridge
a food made by boiling oatmeal to a thick paste

swerved
turned or changed direction suddenly

Comprehension

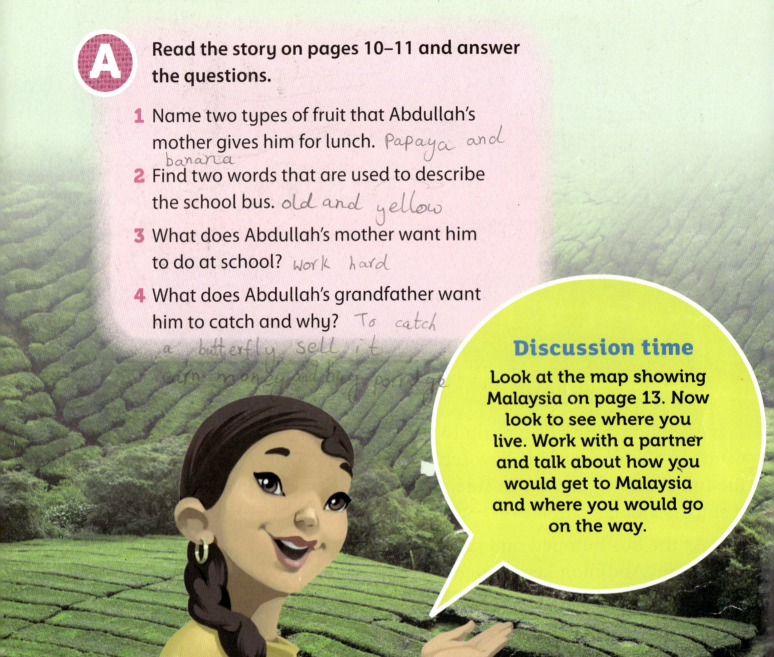

A Read the story on pages 10–11 and answer the questions.

1 Name two types of fruit that Abdullah's mother gives him for lunch. *Papaya and banana*

2 Find two words that are used to describe the school bus. *old and yellow*

3 What does Abdullah's mother want him to do at school? *Work hard*

4 What does Abdullah's grandfather want him to catch and why? *To catch a butterfly sell it earn money and buy porridge*

Discussion time

Look at the map showing Malaysia on page 13. Now look to see where you live. Work with a partner and talk about how you would get to Malaysia and where you would go on the way.

I would travel on a plane to reach Malaysia.

B **What do you think?**

Use phrases from the story to help with your answers.

1 How would you describe the road that leads down to the town from Abdullah's village? *Lots of greenry.*

2 Do you think Abdullah is well behaved? Why? *Yes, because in the story he done nothing wrong.*

3 Why do you think Abdullah's mother tells him to study hard?

4 When Grandfather asks Abdullah to catch a butterfly, he whispers. Why do you think this is? *To sell and buy porridge.*

C **What about you?**

Do you think it is important to work hard at school? Will it help you in the future? Work with a partner and talk about your answer.

Stories with familiar settings (continued)

On his way home from school, Abdullah is looking out of the window of the bus. He sees a beautiful butterfly and decides to get off the bus!

The Butterfly

Abdullah leapt out of his seat. He grabbed up his bag and butterfly net, and stumbled down the aisle.

"Wait," he said urgently. "Let me off."…

5   "You sure?" asked the driver. "It's still a mighty long walk home up the mountain."

But Abdullah nodded adamantly. He wanted to get off, now.

He waved to his friends hanging out the windows
10 and…ran back down the road to where he had seen the butterfly.

…Like a miracle, it was still there, rocking gently on a fern frond. He held his breath in wonder and excitement, because this was the
15 largest, most perfect butterfly of its kind he had ever seen.

…Abdullah stared, almost in a trance, as, with an upward sweep of its brilliant wings, the butterfly
20 launched itself off the plant and into flight.

From *Abdullah's Butterfly* by Janine M. Fraser and Kim Gamble

Word Cloud

adamantly
frond
rocking
trance

Comprehension

 Which three sentences below are true?

1 Abdullah had to stay on the bus.

2 The butterfly landed on a fern. ✓

3 Abdullah was amazed and excited. ✓

4 Abdullah wanted to catch the butterfly. ✓

 What do you think?

Use phrases from the story to help with your answers.

1 Why do you think Abdullah wanted to get off the bus? *Abdullah wanted to get off the bus because he saw a butterfly.*

2 Find words that describe the butterfly. *Large, perfect and brilliant wings.*

• Can you think of any others? *colourful, fluttering and beautiful*

3 How do you think Abdullah felt when the butterfly flew into the air? *I think Abdullah was feeling very excited when he saw the butterfly.*

 **What about you?**

a) What do you think Abdullah did next?

b) What would you have done if you were Abdullah?

a) I think Abdullah will caught the butterfly and took it home.

Challenge

Think of something exciting that happened to you at or after school. Describe it to your friend.

Nouns and adjectives

A **noun** is a **naming** word. Nouns tell us the names of things, places or people.
Examples: bus, school, friend

An **adjective** is a **describing** word. Adjectives give us more information about nouns.
Examples: old, big, funny

Some nouns are called **proper nouns**. These are the names of particular places or people. Proper nouns start with a **capital letter**.
Examples: Abdullah, Malaysia

A Copy the sentences below. Underline the nouns and put a circle around the adjectives.

1 Grandfather eats special porridge.
2 The road to school is long and bumpy.
3 Abdullah sees a beautiful butterfly.

Challenge
Read the story on pages 10–11 and 14 and find two examples of nouns and two examples of adjectives. Write your own sentences using each of the words you find.

B Think of a noun to go with the following adjectives.

1 A yellow _butterfly_
2 A tall _mountain_.
3 A warm _jumper_.

Verbs

A **verb** is a **doing** or **action** word. Verbs tell us what is happening or what someone is doing.

Examples:

The dog **chases** the rabbit across the field.

Leyla **kicks** the ball into the goal.

The verb **to be** is a **being** verb. It tells us what people and things **are**.

Examples:

My journey to school **is** long.

You **are** my friend.

Top Tip

As well as telling us what things are, the verb **to be** tells us what things were and what they will be.

Examples: I was, you were, he will be

A Copy the sentences below and underline the verbs.

1 Abdullah's mother puts his lunch in his satchel.

2 Abdullah listens to his teacher.

3 The driver stops the bus.

B Think of a verb to fill the gaps in the following sentences.

1 Grandfather _is_ hungry.

2 Butterflies _are_ beautiful insects.

3 Abdullah _was_ late for the bus.

Powerful verbs and adjectives

Top Tip

A **thesaurus** helps us to choose more interesting words.

Powerful verbs and **adjectives** make stories more interesting. Look at these sentences.

The mouse ate my cake.
The dinosaur came out of the cave.

Compare them with the sentences below.

The **hungry** mouse **gobbled** up my **favourite** cake.
The **hairy** dinosaur **charged** out of the **dark** cave.

Which do you think are more interesting? The second ones.

A Copy the following sentences and choose the most interesting verb to fill each gap.

1 The bus _climbed_ up the mountain. (climbed, went)
2 Abdullah _grabbed_ his bag. (took, grabbed)
3 Abdullah _stumbled_ down the aisle of the bus. (walked, stumbled)

B Look at the story on pages 10–11 and 14.

1 Find two examples of interesting verbs and two examples of interesting adjectives.

2 Find two nouns that you could describe with an interesting adjective.

New spellings

When learning new spellings, it helps to break the word into **syllables** or chunks.
Example: but-ter-fly

When words are spelt with **two vowels together**, the vowels usually make one sound rather than two.
Examples: r**ea**d, sn**ai**l, s**ou**nd

Top Tip

Words in English are made up of vowels and consonants.
Vowels: a, e, i, o, u
Consonants: The rest of the alphabet

A Here are some of the new words you have learnt in this unit.

**journey satchel floating
porridge weave**

1 Read, say and listen to the words.

2 Write the words down, breaking them into syllables. Which word has only one syllable? *weave*

3 Write a sentence using each of the new words. *The noisy duck floated in the deep, blue water.*

B Look at the new words in A above.

1 Find the vowels in each word.

2 Do any of the words have two vowels together? What sound do the vowels make?

ou, oa and ea

Challenge

Read the story on pages 10–11 and 14. Find two examples of words that are spelt with two vowels together. Write a sentence using each of the words.

Writing a story with a familiar setting
Model writing

The House That Was Sad

One day, for the want of anything better to do, seven-year-old Dolores Li decided to explore the old house at the other end of the village. No one had lived there for years.

She walked past the sign that said 'Keep Out' (Dolores could be rather a disobedient little girl), through the gate and – rather nervously it must be said – made her way towards the old house. What a sad house, she thought. Its windows were broken and the walls were crumbling – and the roof was full of holes. Even the front door flapped back and forth. It sounded just like someone angrily banging a spoon on a table, thought Dolores.

Boldly, she shouted, "Is there anyone there?"

You can imagine her great surprise when a voice replied, "Yes. Do come in."

KEEP OUT

Guided writing

Notice how the story 'The House That Was Sad' uses the following features:

Paragraphs

The writer uses a new paragraph when there is a change of place, time or speaker.

Paragraph 1 *– sets the scene and introduces the main character.*
Paragraph 2 *– there is a new place.*
Paragraph 3 *– someone new speaks.*
Paragraph 4 *– someone new speaks.*

Character

The reader finds out a lot about the main character.

Name – Dolores
Age – seven years old
Personality – bored, disobedient, bold, but sometimes nervous.

Setting

The reader finds out where the story is taking place and some interesting details about the old house, the weather and the noises.

An old house at the other side of the village.
No one has lived in the house for years. Broken windows, crumbling walls, roof with holes, broken front door banging like a spoon on a table.

Writing a story with a familiar setting
Your writing

Finish the story 'The House That Was Sad' with a happy ending. Write a paragraph plan to help you plan your story. In the plan, write a sentence that sums up what is going to happen in each paragraph.

Remember to use a new paragraph when you change any of the following:

Time	*Ten minutes later...*
Place	*They walked into the kitchen.*
Character	*The old lady tiptoed into the room.*
Action	*Suddenly, a door burst open.*
Speaker	*The old man declared, "I want laughter back in this house!"*

Remember to include some details about what the house looks like inside, as well as any noises and smells. You could even bring in what something feels like. It will make your description of the house much more interesting for the reader!

If the house becomes a happy house, you might want to describe the outside so it does not look sad anymore!

Story checklist

When you are writing your story, draw a chart like the one below, which shows the skills you need to show. Check and edit your work as you go along and put ticks in the boxes.

	Yes	No	Sometimes
The story has a happy ending			
New paragraphs are used when there is a change of time, place, action or speaker	✓		
Strong adjectives give information about the characters	✓		
Characters are shown through what they look like, do and say			
The senses are used to describe the house	✓		
Strong verbs are used, e.g cried, kicked			
Spelling is correct	✓		

Top Tip

You might want to ask a friend to help you complete your checklist. Ask your partner if they can think of ways for you to improve your story.

2 Find out how!

"Do as I say, not as I do."
Anon

Let's Talk

1 What is the purpose of the signs in these pictures? Are they warnings or instructions or both?

2 Some warning signs use words and others use pictures. Do you think words or pictures are more effective on signs? Why?

Instruction words

 Look at the words in the Word Cloud and match them to the meanings here.

Word Cloud

instruction
safety
warning

1 Being safe and protected.

2 Something that tells you what to do.

3 Words that tell you to be careful of something.

 Rewrite the following flight safety instructions, putting them in the right order.

1 Unfasten your seatbelt after landing. Instuction 3

2 Fasten your seatbelt ready for Instruction 1 take-off.

3 After take-off, keep your seatbelt Instruction 2 fastened until you see the 'unfasten seatbelt' sign.

 Have you ever used a seatbelt? Was it on a plane, or was it in a car or on a bus? Work with a partner and think of three reasons why it is important to be safe and follow safety signs and rules.

25

Instructions

The instructions below explain how to make a mask using a balloon and tissue paper.

From Balloon to Mask

Materials

Small cardboard box	Pin
Balloon pump	Modelling clay
Coloured tissue paper	Sticky tape
Balloon	Scissors
Glue mixture	Paintbrush

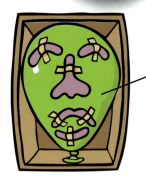

Make sure the balloon is roughly the size of your own head.

1 <u>Blow</u> up a balloon and place it in a shoebox to keep it stable. The balloon will form the basic shape of your mask.

2 <u>Use</u> modelling clay to make the eyebrows, nose, mouth and chin. <u>Attach</u> these shapes to the balloon with sticky tape.

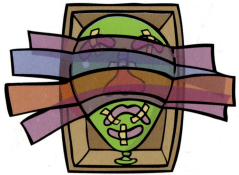

3 <u>Cut</u> long strips of differently coloured tissue paper and stick them over the whole face area using the glue mixture.

4 Build up the balloon with lots of layers of tissue paper. Leave to dry overnight and the tissue paper will turn hard and shiny.

Fabulous faces

Remove the balloon and modelling clay from your mask. Now you have your very own multi-coloured tissue-paper mask to display on your wall!

Pop the balloon with a pin, but be careful, it may pop with a loud bang!

Glossary

create
produce or make something

layer
a single thickness of a material

tissue paper
very thin paper which you can almost see through

Stripy mask

Why not cut out holes in the eyes and mouth so you can wear the mask? Your friends won't recognize you with it on!

Try using layers of colours down the mask to create a stripy look.

The eyebrows and other features are raised.

Pierce the mask with a pencil before you cut out the eyes and mouth.

From *Great Art Attack Stuff with Neil Buchanan*, Dorling Kindersley

27

Comprehension

A Read the instructions on pages 26–27 and answer the questions.

1 What kind of box will help to keep the balloon stable? *A shoe-box.*

2 What is the modelling clay used for? *To make the eyes, nose and mouth.*

3 In which step is the sticky tape used? *To stick the modelling clay to the balloon.*

4 How can the tissue paper be used to give a stripy effect? *Cut tissue paper in very thin papers.*

Discussion time

In groups discuss whether you read instructions or try to do things for yourself. If you buy a new game do you read the instructions? Give reasons for your answers.

B **What do you think?**

Use phrases from the instructions to help with your answers.

1 Find six verbs used in the instructions that tell readers what to do.

2 How do the instructions show which step to carry out next?

3 Do you think the diagrams are helpful? Give reasons for your answer.

4 Are the instructions fiction or non-fiction? How do you know?

C **What about you?**

What sort of mask would you like to make? What materials would you need to make it?

29

Instructions (continued)

Read the following instructions for how to make a grass head, using a pair of tights, some garden compost and grass seed.

🔵 Make a Grass Head

Word Cloud
compost
decorate
elastic band
pipe cleaners
tights

You will need:
Pair of clean, thin tights
Compost
2–3 teaspoons of grass seed
Elastic band
Items for decorating the head, such as stick-on eyes and pipe cleaners
Small pot

1 First, cut a piece from the foot end of the tights, about 20 cm (8 inches) long.

2 Next, put a little compost into the toe end and sprinkle in the grass seed.

3 Then, fill the foot with compost to make a ball about the size of a tennis ball.

4 Tie a knot at the open end to stop the compost coming out.

5 Draw a little compost out at the 'front' of the head and tie an elastic band round to make a nose.

6 Finally, decorate your grass head, for example with stick-on eyes and glasses made from pipe cleaners.

Answer for Question (B)

To make the grass grow, pour some water into a small pot. Rest the head on the pot with the tied end hanging in the water. The water will gradually soak through to the grass seed. The grass will start growing after about a week. Add more water to the pot at least every two days.

Comprehension

A **Which three sentences are true?**

1 You do not need to add water.

2 A grass head is made from tights, compost and grass seeds. ✓

3 The grass will grow after about a week. ✓

4 You can add eyes and glasses to the grass head. ✓

B **What do you think?**

1 Find three words that the writer uses to show the start of a new stage.

2 What is the elastic band used for?

The elastic band is used for the nose.

3 Why is it important to water the grass head? Because that will help the grass to grow.

C **What about you?**

How would you decorate your grass head? Write some step-by-step instructions for how to add the decorations.

Challenge

Work in pairs and take it in turns to give your partner instructions for how to draw a decorated grass head. At the end, look at your pictures. Were the instructions good? How could they be improved?

31

Sentences

Look at the following two groups of words:

I **made** a mask at school today.
mask at school today.

The first group of words is a **sentence.** It contains a **verb** ('made') and **makes sense on its own.** The second group of words does not make sense on its own and does not contain a verb. It is not a sentence.

Top Tip
Sentences begin with a **capital letter** and end with a **full stop.**

Challenge
Look at the road sign here. Write a sentence explaining what the sign means.

 A Look at the three groups of words below. Copy *only* the sentences and underline the verbs.

1 Johan <u>followed</u> the instructions. = sentence
2 ready for <u>take</u> off = not sentence
3 <u>Fasten</u> your seatbelts. = not sentence

 B Rewrite the following words in the right order to make sentences. Remember to use capital letters and full stops.

1 the cake in <u>leave</u> for the oven 40 minutes = Leave the cake in the oven for 40 minutes.
2 ingredients the of all recipe the listed
 listed the recipe of

PENGUINS
CROSSING

SLOW

Questions and commands

Some sentences are **questions**. Questions often begin with question words such as **what**, **where**, **who** and **why**. Questions always end with a question mark (**?**).
Example: What time is it?

Some sentences are **commands**. Commands start with an **imperative** or 'bossy' **verb**. We use these verbs to give commands. Commands sometimes end with an exclamation mark (**!**).
Example: Look both ways!

Top Tip

Exclamation marks can be used at the end of sentences to show surprise, excitement or force.
Example: I don't believe it!

Challenge

Look at the instruction text on pages 26–27. Find three examples of 'bossy' or imperative verbs and use them in your own sentences.

 Rewrite the following sentences, using a command verb from below to fill the gaps.

jump run kick

1 Jump over the fence!
2 Kick the ball into the goal!
3 Run for the bus!

 Add capital letters and the correct punctuation marks to the sentences below.

1 Where are you going?
2 It is so windy today!
3 Have you seen the scissors?

Tenses

We use different **tenses** to say **when** something happens.

We use a verb in the **present tense** to tell us about things that are happening **now**.

Examples:
The horse **jumps** over the fence.
The horse **is jumping** over the fence.

We use a verb in the **past tense** to tell us about things that happened **in the past**. Verbs in the past tense often end with **ed**.

Example: The horse **jumped** over the fence.

Top Tip

When we use a present tense with 'he', 'she', 'it' or the name of a person or thing, we must remember to add an 's' to the verb.

Examples:
She plays basketball every Saturday.

Harshil eats the apple.

 A Find the verbs in the following sentences. Write down whether the verbs are in the present or past tense.

1 The penguins <u>dived</u> into the sea. *past*

2 Ahmed is <u>cleaning</u> his teeth. = *present*

3 Rahini and Anna <u>listened</u> to the music. = *past*

 B Rewrite the sentences changing the verbs to the past tense.

1 The parrot *landed* lands on the branch of the tree.

2 The referee *picked* picks up the ball.

3 Aisha *waited* waits for the bus to arrive.

Aroush (3.1)

Adding –ed and –ing to verbs

We can often add **–ed** or **–ing** to verbs without changing the rest of the spelling.
Examples: shout, shout**ed**, shout**ing**

When a verb ends in **e**, we drop the **e** before adding **–ed** or **–ing**.
Examples: danc**e**, danc**ed**, danc**ing**

When a verb ends in a short vowel followed by a consonant, we **double** the consonant before adding **–ed** or **–ing**.
Examples: slip, slip**ped**, slip**ping**

Top Tip

Short vowels have a short, snappy sound. Saying the words out loud will help you to know whether the vowel is short. *Examples:* dr**o**p, sk**i**p, gr**a**b

A Add *–ing* or *–ed* to the verbs below and use them to fill the gaps.

rest   wash   eat

1 My uncle _washed_ his car last Sunday.

2 Amy is _eating_ a piece of fruit.

3 The lion is _resting_ in the sun.

B Find the misspelled words in the sentences below and rewrite the words with the correct spellings.

1 Amy is bakeing a cake.   *baking*

2 The car stoped so the children could cross *stopped* the road.

3 The fish are swiming in the sea.   *swimming*

Writing instructions
Model writing

How to Clean Your Teeth

What you will need:
Toothbrush
Tube of toothpaste
Glass
Water
Towel

1 Get ready...
First, pick up your toothbrush and hold it firmly in one hand. Take the tube of toothpaste in your other hand. Remove the top and squeeze a small amount of toothpaste onto the brush. Put the top back on the toothpaste tube.

2 Get brushing...
Next, brush all your teeth for two minutes.

3 Get sorted...
Then, fill a glass half full with water, and use this to rinse your mouth. Spit the water from your mouth into the sink. Turn on the tap so that the 'toothpaste water' is rinsed away and wash your toothbrush under the tap.

4 Finally...
Dry your mouth with a towel. Your teeth should now be clean!

Guided writing

Instructions explain how to make something or how to do something. Notice how the instructions 'How to Clean Your Teeth' use the following features:

- A title that states clearly the goal of the instructions.
- A list of things you will need.
- A clearly numbered list of steps, with each step set out on a new line.
- Command (bossy) verbs near the beginning of each instruction.
- Short, clear sentences.
- Diagrams to help make the instructions clear.
- A summing up of what should have been achieved, such as 'Your teeth should now be clean.'

Top Tip

Instructions often include words such as 'First', 'Next', 'Then' and 'Finally' at the start of each new stage. These words help the reader know a new stage has started.

Writing instructions
Your writing

Write your own set of instructions. These could be on how to do one of the following:

- Sweep a floor
- Get from school to home
- Make a cup of tea
- Operate a computer game
- Play a game
- Make a model aeroplane
- Do a handstand or cartwheel
- Hold a successful birthday party
- Make some Mexican tortillas

Whatever you choose, remember to:

- Have a clear aim. What is it someone will be able to do at the end if they follow the instructions?

- Use some diagrams to help make the instructions clear.

Instructions checklist

Make up your own checklist of what you think you need in order to write a successful set of instructions. It should look something like this.

	Yes	No	Sometimes
Include a title stating the aim of the instructions	✓		
Provide a list of things you will need	✓		
Number each step and put each new step on a new line	✓		
Use command verbs at the beginning of each sentence			
Use short, clear sentences	✓		
Include diagrams			
Sum up what should have been achieved			

3 Our sensational senses

"Children, like animals, use all their senses to discover the world."
Eudora Welty

Let's Talk

1 What words would you use to describe what the girl in this picture can see, feel and smell?

2 We have five senses, sight, hearing, taste, touch and smell. Which is your favourite sense?

Senses words

Word Cloud

flavour
noise
scent

A Look at the words in the Word Cloud and match them to the meanings here.

1 A smell that you sense with your nose.
2 A sound that you hear with your ears.
3 A taste that you sense in your mouth.

B Copy out this table and put the words into the right column. Some of the words might fit in more than one column.

wet red delicious crunchy purple
loud cold sweet tasty fruity

See	Hear	Taste	Touch	Smell
yellow	quiet	salty	soft	scented

C Work with a partner and take it in turns to talk about your favourite food. Think of words to describe how the food looks, tastes, smells, feels and sounds when you eat it.

41

Poems about the senses

This poem by Roger McGough is about a mysterious man who steals sounds.

The Sound Collector

A stranger called this morning
Dressed all in black and grey
Put every sound into a bag
And carried them away

5 The whistling of the kettle
The turning of the lock
The purring of the kitten
The ticking of the clock

The popping of the toaster
10 The crunching of the flakes
When you spread the marmalade
The scraping noise it makes

Word Cloud

drain
grill
scraping
swishing
whistling

Tick Tock!

whistle!

hiss!

POP!

Bread

Purr!

crunch!

The hissing of the frying pan
The ticking of the grill
15 The bubbling of the bathtub
As it starts to fill

The drumming of the raindrops
On the window-pane
When you do the washing up
20 The gurgle of the drain

The crying of the baby
The squeaking of the chair
The swishing of the curtain
The creaking of the stair.

25 A stranger called this morning
He didn't leave his name
Left us only silence
Life will never be the same again.

Roger McGough

Glossary

marmalade
a sweet spread usually made from oranges, which people eat on toast

stranger
somebody you do not know

Gurgle!

scrape!
crape! Waaaa!

CORN FLAKES

Comprehension

A Read the poem on pages 42–43 and answer the questions.

1 What time of day was it when the stranger called?
The stranger was called, This Morning.
2 Find the word in the poem that describes the sound of raindrops on a window. *The word that decribes the raindrops is drumming*
3 Make a list of the words that rhyme in the poem. Can you see a pattern? ①*grey away* ②*clock lock* ③*floor snore*
They all end in same sound ⑤*drain window pane*
4 What did the stranger leave behind? ⑥*chair stair*
Silience

crunch!
hiss!
purr!

B What do you think?

Use phrases from the poem to help with your answer.

1 Which sounds in the poem do you like the most? Are there any you dislike?

2 Which words in the poem are the most effective?

3 Can you think of any other sounds the sound collector could have taken?

4 At the end of the poem, why does the poet say life will never be the same?

C What about you?

How would you feel if the world became silent? Which sounds would you miss the most? Are there any sounds you would not miss?

Discussion time

Imagine the sound collector had come to your school. Think of four words to describe the sounds he might have taken. In a group, compare your words.

Poems about the senses (continued)

This poem by John Foster is about a young fox that uses its senses to find out if it is safe to leave its home.

Word Cloud

creeps
danger
peer
sniffs

The Young Fox

At night, the young fox pokes its head
Out of its den beneath the shed.

It listens with its pointed ears
To hear if there is danger near.

5   Its sharp nose sniffs the air and tells
If there are any dangerous smells.

Its sharp eyes peer from left to right
Watching for movements in the night.

If it senses it's safe, then up it leaps
10 And off across the fields it creeps.

John Foster

Comprehension

 A **Which three sentences below are true?**

1 The fox lives in a shed.

2 The fox listens for sounds of danger. ✓

3 The fox has a good sense of smell. ✓

4 If it is safe, the fox creeps across the fields. ✓

 B **What do you think?**

Use phrases from the poem to help with your answer.

It's sharp nose sniffs the air
It's sharp eyes pearl Left to right.

1 Which three senses does the fox use to check for danger? *It listens with it's pointed ears.*

2 Do you think the fox has good hearing? Why?
Yes, because it has pointy ear and can turn it's ear where noise is coming from.

3 Why do you think the poet chose the word 'creeps' in the last verse? *Incase there is a preditar he doesn't run he creeps.*

4 Which words in the poem do you think are most effective? Give reasons for your answer.

Sniffs, listens, watching because they describe the for in it's best form.

 C **What about you?**

Why do you think the young fox needs to check for danger before leaving its den?

Incase there is a preditar

Challenge

With a partner, practise reading the poem 'The Young Fox' aloud. Take it in turns to read the verses. Express yourself as you read! Have fun. You can pretend to do the fox's actions as you read the poem.

Prefixes

A **prefix** is a group of letters that can be added to the beginning of a word to change its meaning.

Two common prefixes are **un-** and **dis-**. Both of these prefixes mean **not**.

Examples:
dis + like = dislike (not like)
un + happy = unhappy (not happy)

Top Tip

Prefixes are always placed before a **root word** to make a new word with a different meaning.

Example:
Root word – happy

un + happy = unhappy

A Add the prefix *un-* or *dis-* to the following words to make new words with the opposite meaning.

trust   un**kind**   un**safe**
un**lucky**   dis **appear**   dis **allow**

B Copy out the following sentences. Add the prefix *un-* or *dis-* to the words below and use the new words to fill the gaps.

like tidy comfortable

1 Ahmed thought his new shoes were very _uncofortable_ .

2 Kofi and Tom both _dislike_ bananas.

3 Mary's bedroom is always _untidy_ .

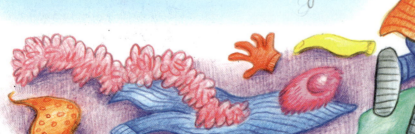

More prefixes

A The prefix *re-* means 'again'. Rewrite the following sentences, adding the prefix *re-* to the verbs.

1 The family visited their favourite beach. *revisited*
2 Kofi filled his glass with water. *refilled*
3 The football team arranged the game. *rearranged*

Top Tip

Knowing about **prefixes** and **root words** is useful for spelling. Prefixes form separate syllables, so they help you break down words into smaller parts.

B The prefix *pre-* means 'before' and the prefix *de-* means 'remove' or 'make opposite'.

1 Add the prefix *pre-* or *de-* to the following words to make a new word.

pre **historic** *de* **frost** *pre* **view** *de* **value**

2 Write a sentence using each of the new words you made in 1.

3 How have the prefixes changed the meaning of the words in 1?

C Use a dictionary to find two new words that begin with the prefixes *un-, dis-, de-, re-* and *pre-*. Working with a partner, take it in turns to test each other on the spelling and meaning of the words.

49

Writing a play script
Model writing

Read the conversation below. In the first two paragraphs, the words that are spoken are in blue. Notice that there are speech marks (" ") around the words. The words in orange describe *how* the words are spoken and the actions of the characters. We show what we are thinking by how we talk, the expressions on our faces and how we move. The names of the characters are in green.

Lost Shoes

"I can't find my shoes!" wailed seven-year-old George Green, desperately searching under his bed. "I've looked everywhere!"

"They must be somewhere, George. You would have taken them off last night before you went to bed," said George's dad, scratching his head. "Let's search the room together. Are you ready? On top of the bed?"

"No," said George.

"Under your desk?"

"No," said George.

"Behind your computer?"

"No," said George.

"Then," Dad declared, "you are just going to have to go to the birthday party with no shoes on. Let's go. You don't want to be late. Mum's waiting downstairs to take you."

"Perhaps no one will notice," George muttered, as he glanced down at his bright green socks. He sighed, "What shall I do?"

Guided writing

Change the conversation on page 50 into a play script. Use the following features in your play script.

Characters

In play scripts, the speaker (highlighted in green in the text on page 50) is written in bold on the left-hand side of the page.

Dialogue

The words inside the speech marks on page 50 (highlighted in blue) are the words the characters say. There is no need to use speech marks in a play script.

Stage directions

Words such as 'scratching his head' on page 50 (highlighted in orange) can be used as instructions for the actors. Stage directions tell the actors what to do on stage and how to say their words. Put the stage directions in brackets.

The opening is done for you:

George (*desperately searching under the bed*) I can't find my shoes! I've looked everywhere!

Dad (*scratching his head*) They must be somewhere, George.

Your writing

Add your own ending to the play script. Does George find his shoes or go to the party with no shoes? Or does he wear his slippers or someone else's shoes? You decide. You might have to introduce new characters, such as George's mum and sister.

Revise and check **1**

Vocabulary

1 Choose the correct word to complete the sentences.

  a A tiny kitten was _purring_ softly on the sofa. (purring, swishing)

  b The driver noticed the _pedestrian_ and stopped the car just in time. (butterfly, pedestrian)

  c There was a _warning_ sign by the side of the road. (warning, scraping)

2 Match the prefixes to the root words and write a sentence for each of the new words.

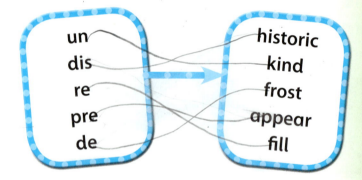

un · historic
dis · kind
re · frost
pre · appear
de · fill

Punctuation

1 Rewrite the text below with the correct punctuation (capital letters, full stops, question marks and exclamation marks).

Ddolores crept up to the old house she heard a whistling noise near the door it was the strangest sound she had ever heard what was it what should she do?

Grammar

1 Copy the following sentences. Underline the nouns, circle the verbs and tick the adjectives.

a The artist created a beautiful sculpture.

b The noisy school children shrieked all afternoon.

c Robbie is washing the sticky pots.

Spelling

1 Copy the table below and put the following words in the right columns.

cyclist delicious flavour butterfly porridge marmalade

Three syllable words	Two syllable words
dangerous	journey

2 Copy the sentences below and complete the words with two vowels that make a single sound.

ea ai ou

a A snail crept onto the plant.

b It didn't make a sound.

c The spider started to weave a web.

4 Traditional tales

"We do everything as well as we can."
Traditional Balinese saying

Let's Talk

1 Look at these pictures of children from Bali, Indonesia. What do you think is happening in the pictures? Would you like to take part in a traditional performance?

2 Think of three traditions in your country.

Traditional words

Look at the words in the Word Cloud and match them to the meanings here.

1 A very old story that has been told for many years.

2 A big celebration.

3 An idea or custom that is passed down from one generation to another.

Copy the following sentences and use the words below to fill the gaps.

tales   instruments   ceremonies

Bali has many ___tales___ and legends. Dancers often

act out the stories in special ___ceremonies___.

Musicians make music with traditional ___instruments___.

Traditional tales and legends often involve imaginary animals and animals that can speak. Do you know any traditional tales like this? Tell a partner the story.

Traditional tales

This story comes from the island of Bali, Indonesia. It is about Bawang. Her name means 'red onion'. She is very sweet-tempered, and red onions are sweet, so that is how she got her name.

A Balinese Folk Tale

Every wash-day Bawang went down to the river with a basket of clothes. One day, as usual, she bathed herself in the fast-flowing water, then reached for a sarong to wash. But
5   the basket had disappeared!

"Oh no!" gasped poor Bawang. "Mother will be so cross if I have lost all our clothes."

Bawang realized she must have placed the basket too near the water's edge and that it had
10   tipped in, so she ran downstream as fast as her feet would carry her, to see if she could find it.

Bawang ran and ran, but still she could not see the basket. Tired out, she stopped to catch her breath. Two fish popped their heads out
15   of the water to see who was puffing and panting so.

"Oh, fish, have you seen my basket of clothes in the river?" she asked.

"No sister, we have not seen your basket,"
20   the fish replied.

Word Cloud

downstream
gasped
panting
puffing

Bawang ran on, tears running down her cheeks. She saw some frogs sitting on the river bank.

"Oh frogs," sobbed Bawang, "have you seen
5 my basket of clothes float by?"

"We regret, sister, that we have seen no basket of clothes," croaked the frogs.

Bawang ran on further until she saw some crabs sunning themselves by the water.

0 "Oh, good crabs, please, you must have seen my basket of clothes passing by on the river?"

"No," replied the crabs. "We have not seen your clothes; but don't cry so, it's not such a loss. *We* don't need clothes."

From *Folk Tales of the World* retold by Gini Wade

Glossary

catch your breath
to stop and rest when you are short of breath

regret
to be sorry

sarong
a piece of cloth worn by people in Bali

sunning
sitting in the sun

Comprehension

A Read the story on pages 56–57 and answer the questions.

1 Which three kinds of animals did Bawang talk to? She talked to the animals fish, frog and crab

2 Why did the fish pop their heads out of the water? The fish pop their head out of the water to see who was puffing and panting.

3 Where were the frogs sitting? By the river bank

4 Why did the crabs tell Bawang not to cry? Because he said, "We don't need clothes."

What do you think?

Use phrases from the story to help with
your answer.

1 Why do you think Bawang was so unhappy
when she saw that the basket had gone? *She was going
to be in so much trouble from her mum!*

2 Find three strong verbs in the story that the
author has used instead of 'said'.

3 Find the phrase that describes how quickly
Bawang ran along the river bank. Do you
think this phrase is effective? Why?

4 Write two sentences to describe what we
know about Bawang's character.

C **What about you?**

How would you feel if you were Bawang?
What would you do?

Discussion time

Stories can sometimes
make us form pictures in
our minds. Work with a
partner and describe the
pictures this story makes
you think of.

Traditional tales (continued)

A Golden Bird

But Bawang could not stop crying. In fact, she sat on the bank and cried all the more. She saw a great golden bird sitting in the tree above her and she sang to him:

5   "Golden bird, golden bird,

I am so miserable I no longer wish to live,

Come peck me till I die."

The bird was called Tjilalongan and he was not an ordinary bird. He flew down
10 and pecked Bawang's head, but instead of blood, gold flowers appeared in her hair. Then he pecked her body and her sarong turned to gold. Bawang was amazed and overjoyed. She jumped
15 up and cried,

"Now I can sell the gold and buy my family new clothes! Oh great bird, how can I ever thank you?"

"There is no need," replied
20 Tjilalongan. "I have been watching over you, Bawang, and you are a good child. This is your reward." And with this he flew off.

From *Folk Tales of the World* retold by Gini Wade

Word Cloud

overjoyed
pecked
reward

Comprehension

A Which three sentences below are true?

1 Bawang sang to Tjilalongan. ✓

2 Tjilalongan was an ordinary bird.

3 Bawang's sarong turned to gold. ✓

4 Gold flowers appeared in Bawang's hair. ✓

B **What do you think?**

Use phrases from the story to help you.

1 Why do you think the bird gave Bawang a reward? Because it had been watching Bawang, and she was a good girl so she got a reward

2 What did the bird do to help Bawang? The bird gave her gold.

3 Why was Bawang so happy when her sarong turned to gold? Because then with that gold she can buy her parents clothes!

4 Did Bawang want anything for herself? Explain your answer. No.

C **What about you?**

Bawang felt very upset when she lost the basket of clothes. Have you ever lost something? Did you find it? Talk with a partner about how it made you feel.

Challenge
This is not the end of the folk tale. What do you think happens next? Make up your own ending for the story.

Synonyms

A **synonym** is a word that has the same meaning or nearly the same meaning as another word. Synonyms can be **nouns**, **adjectives** or **verbs**.

Examples:
noise, sound
laugh, giggle
big, large

Top Tip

If you want to find a synonym for a word, look in a **thesaurus.** You will also find other words with similar meanings. You can use the words to make your writing more interesting.

Challenge

Look up the words 'good', 'bad', 'big' and 'little' in a thesaurus. For each word, find another word with a similar meaning. Write a sentence using each of the new words you find.

A Copy the following words and choose the correct synonym from the words in brackets.

1 honest (trust, truthful, believe)
2 teach (instruct, lesson, tutor)
 or
3 mistake (wrong, error, false)

B Rewrite the following sentences, replacing the words in bold with a synonym below.

assist   angry   overjoyed

1 Bawang thought her mother would be **cross**. *angry*
2 The frogs could not **help** Bawang. *assist*
3 Bawang was **happy** when her sarong turned to gold. *overjoyed*

More interesting words for 'said'

When text includes dialogue, or words spoken by a person, we often use the verb **said**.

Example:
"My basket has disappeared!" **said** Bawang.

We can make our writing more interesting by choosing another word instead of 'said'.

Example:
"My basket has disappeared!" **sobbed** Bawang.

In the following sentences, change the word 'said' to one of the more interesting verbs below.

whispered   screamed   laughed

1 "That puppy is so funny," Fatima said. *laughed*
2 "Don't wake the baby!" Lucas said. *whispered*
3 "Oh no, I hate insects!" said Rahini. *screamed*

Top Tip

Read the sentences in exercise A out loud. Notice how the word we choose changes the way we say the sentence.

Look at the verbs below and write a sentence using each of the words.

announce   ask   explain   roar   shout

Speech marks

When we write down the words that someone speaks in a text, we put **speech marks** (" ") before and after the words that are spoken.

Example: Bawang asked, **"**Have you seen my basket?**"**

Top Tip

We use a capital letter for the first word of each sentence that is spoken. A new line is used when a new person speaks.

A Copy the following sentences and add in the missing speech marks.

1 Have you seen my school bag? asked Peter.

2 Throw the ball to me! shouted Rahim.

3 The waiter said, Here is your orange juice.

B Imagine a scene in a restaurant. Copy out the sentences below, filling in the words that each person might say.

1 The waiter asked, "_____?"

2 Ahmed replied, "_____."

64

Speech punctuation

When we use **speech marks**, we put a **full stop** or a **comma** just before the closing speech mark.

Examples:

Leyla said, "I am going to the aquarium on Sunday to see the fish**."**

"My Mum said she would take me**,"** Leyla explained.

Some sentences need a **question mark** or an **exclamation mark** at the end.

Examples:

"Will you come with me**?"** Leyla asked.

Jane replied, "I would love to**!"**

A Copy the sentences below, adding a comma or full stop before the closing speech mark.

1 "We will pick you up at 11 o'clock_" said Leyla.
2 Jane answered, "I will make sure I am ready_"
3 "We will be back by 4 o'clock_" added Leyla.

B Rewrite these sentences adding in the missing speech punctuation.

1 Jane asked Can I go with Leyla to the aquarium
2 Yes, of course exclaimed Mum.
3 I cannot wait to go said Leyla.

Rewriting a traditional tale

Model writing

Traditional stories are often stories written a long time ago. Read through this modernized beginning to the traditional tale 'Goldilocks and the Three Bears.'

Goldilocks and the Three Bears

It was the usual hectic Monday morning for the Bear family at number 5 Foxhole Avenue.

"Dad, I can't find my school bag!" shrieked John Bear. John was 5 years old and had just started at the local school. He was a rather forgetful young bear.

"It's by the television, where you left it last night," Dad shouted back, while trying to put on his coat. "Come on, Mum and I are going to be late for work if you don't get a move on. We don't even have enough time to eat our porridge!"

With that, they all bundled out of the house, into the car and sped off – forgetting to lock the door behind them...

Glossary

bundled out
went quickly together

get a move on
hurry

hectic
busy

Guided writing

In the traditional story of 'Goldilocks and the Three Bears', Goldilocks gets lost in a forest. She finds a house and walks in. She tastes three bowls of porridge and sits in three chairs. Finally, she falls asleep in one of three beds. It is then that the three bears return…

Notice how the modernized opening of the story, on page 66, includes some features of the original story. Other features have changed.

Feature	Traditional story	Modernized version
Opening	*'Once upon a time', 'Long, long ago' or 'One day'*	*'It was the usual hectic Monday morning…'*
Characters	*Three bears*	*John Bear goes to school and Mum and Dad have jobs.*
Setting	*A house in a forest*	*A house in a street*
Plot	*Three bears go for a walk in the forest while their porridge cools down. They leave the door unlocked.*	*The bears leave the house in a rush, leaving the door unlocked.*

Top Tip

Traditional tales often include animal characters that can talk. The number three is also important.

Rewriting a traditional tale
Your writing

Write your own updated version of a traditional tale. You can either choose your own tale to update, or continue with the modernized version of the 'Goldilocks and the Three Bears' story. Whichever you choose, start by making a plan.

Top Tip

Remember to start a new paragraph when there is a change of time, place, character or action.

1 List some of the typical features of traditional stories that you plan to include.

Example: talking animals and things that happen in threes.

2 List some modern features that you plan to include.

Example: John Bear goes to school.

3 Make your story four to five paragraphs long. Write a sentence saying what will happen in each paragraph.

Example: The bears return home and see that John Bear's porridge has been eaten.

4 Include some speech or dialogue.

Example: "We don't even have enough time to eat our porridge!"

Traditional story checklist

Copy out a chart like the one below to help you write a good story!
Check your work as you go along and put ticks on your chart.

	Yes	No	Sometimes
Includes modern features	✓		
Dialogue is used to move the story along			
A new paragraph starts when there is a change in time, speaker and action	✓		
Speech punctuation is used correctly	✓		
Interesting words are used instead of 'said'			
Spelling is correct			

Keep in touch!

"Never write a letter while you are angry."
Old Chinese proverb

Let's Talk

1 Look at this picture. What do you think is happening? Why do you think this boy looks happy?

2 Have you ever written a letter or an email? Why did you write it?

Using words

 Look at the words in the Word Cloud and match them to the meanings here.

1 A place where you buy stamps or post a letter.

2 Letters and other mail items that are sent in a plane.

3 The details of where someone lives.

Word Cloud

address
air mail
post office

 Copy the sentences below. Use the correct words to fill the gaps.

stamp   envelope   handwriting   pen

It is fun to get a letter in the post.
I open the _____ and tear off the
_____. I keep it for my collection.
My grandmother always uses _____ and
ink when she writes to me. Sometimes it
is hard to read her _____ !

 Do you like emails or letters best?
Work with a partner and talk about
what is the same and what is different
about sending a letter and an email.

71

Letters

The letters on this page and page 73 come from a book about a girl whose full name is Clarice Bean Tuesday. In the story, Clarice and her friend Betty write to the author of their favourite books.

Letter to Patricia Maplin Stacey

Dear Patricia F Maplin Stacey,

We are avidish readers of the Ruby Redfort series and we have read all of them at least once. What we would like to know is when is the next Ruby Redfort book coming out and what will it be called?

Also, on page a hundred and 6, chapter eight of Run for it Ruby why did the arch villain Hogtrotter not double-check that he had locked the cellar door?

And also, on page 33 you said Ruby was wearing her glasses and then later on you say she couldn't see well because she didn't have her reading glasses.

Eagerly awaiting your reply.

Betty P Moody and Clarice Bean Tuesday.

p.s. We think you should write a bit faster.

From *Utterly Me, Clarice Bean* by Lauren Child

72

Letter to Clarice and Betty

Dear Betty and Clarace,

Thank you for your kind enquiry. In answer to your question, the next Ruby book will be published this autumn.

The title is yet to be announced.

Patricia F Maplin Stacey hopes you continue to enjoy her books and wishes you happy reading!

Yours truly,

Patricia F Maplin Stacey

Creator of the Ruby Redfort Collection.

(Details of the fan club are listed on the Ruby Redfort website.)

Word Cloud

creator
enquiry
published
truly

Comprehension

 Read the letters on pages 72 and 73 and answer the questions.

1 What is the name of the villain in the book *Run for it Ruby*?

2 What word do Clarice and Betty use to address the author at the beginning of the letter?

3 In which paragraph do Clarice and Betty explain the main purpose of their letter?

4 What two questions do Clarice and Betty ask the author about her next book?

What do you think?

Use phrases from the letters to help with your answers.

1 How do we know that Clarice and Betty want to read more books about Ruby Redfort?

2 Do you think the author wrote the reply to Clarice and Betty herself? Why?

3 Do you think the author's reply answers all of Clarice and Betty's questions? Explain your answer.

4 Can you find a spelling mistake in the author's reply?

 What about you?

Who would you like to write a fan letter to? Think of three questions you would like to ask them.

Discussion time

Talk about the different ways of ending a letter, such as 'Yours sincerely', 'Yours faithfully', 'With love from', and 'Best wishes'. Write them on the board and discuss when you would use them.

Letters (continued)

The letter below was written by Roald Dahl to his mother. He wrote it when he was a young boy and living away from home at boarding school. Roald Dahl grew up to become a successful author.

Word Cloud

boarding school
masters
springs
stamp album

23rd Sept

Dear Mama

I am having a lovely time here.

We play football every day here. The beds have no springs. Will you send my stamp album, and quite a lot of swaps. The masters are very nice. I've got all my clothes now, and a belt, and, tie, and a school Jersey.

Love from

Boy

Comprehension

Which three sentences below are true?

1 Roald Dahl's mother calls him 'Boy'.

2 The beds in the school are comfortable.

3 Roald thinks the teachers at his school are nice.

4 Roald collects stamps.

What do you think?

Use phrases from the letter to help with your answer.

1 Why do you think Roald is writing to his mother?

2 Find two sentences in the letter that show that Roald likes his school.

3 Roald asks his mother to send him some 'swaps'. What do you think these are and what will he do with them?

4 Do you think there is anything that Roald does not like about his school? Explain your answer.

What about you?

How would you describe your school in a letter to a friend or family member?

Challenge

Think of a place that you have visited that you liked. Describe what you liked about it in a letter to a friend. Was there anything you didn't like about it?

Suffixes

A **suffix** is a group of letters that can be added to the end of a word. Adding a suffix changes the meaning of the word.

The suffix **–ful** means 'full of something'.
Example: power + ful = powerful (full of power)

The suffix **–less** means 'without something'.
Example: taste + less = tasteless (without taste)

 A Add the suffix –*ful* to the following words. How does the suffix change the meaning?

hope pain thank harm

hopful painless thankfully harmless

Top Tip

When the suffixes –*ful* and –*less* are added to nouns they change the nouns into adjectives.

 B Copy the sentences below and add the suffixes –*ful* or –*less* to complete the gaps.

1 Oh no, I have broken the glass. How care<u>less</u> of me!
2 That's a wonder<u>full</u> birthday cake!
3 My pen is broken so it is use<u>less</u>!
4 My kite is very colour<u>ful</u>.

 C Write a sentence using each of the words you made in A.

Suffixes

The suffix **–ly** is often used in words that describe **how** or **in what way** something is done.

Example: slow + ly = slowly (done in a slow way)

 A Rewrite the sentences below. Use the following words to fill the gaps, adding the suffix *–ly*.

safe   quick   happy

1 After a long journey, they were glad to get home <u>safely</u>.

2 The children were playing <u>happily</u> on the beach.

3 The monkey <u>quickly</u> climbed to the top of the tree to pick a banana.

B Match the words to the correct suffix and write a sentence using each word.

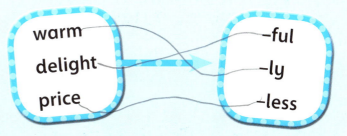

warm   –ful
delight   –ly
price   –less

Singular and plural

We can write nouns in the **singular** or the **plural**. Singular means there is **just one**. Plural means there are **more than one**.

Many singular nouns are made into plural nouns by adding an **s**.
Example: apple → apples

We add **es** to singular nouns that end in **ch**, **sh**, **ss** or **x**.
Example: fox → foxes

A Change the following nouns into plural nouns by adding *s* or *es*.

| pencil | rabbit | book |
| glass | watch | dish |

Top Tip

When you use a plural noun with a verb, the verb must be plural, too.

B Rewrite the sentences below. Fill the gaps using plurals of the following words.

flower   dog   beach

1 We visited two _____ on our holiday.
2 The _____ were barking loudly.
3 The field was full of pretty _____.

Challenge

Look at the letters on pages 72 and 73 . Find two examples of singular nouns and two examples of plural nouns. Write four sentences, using one of the nouns in each sentence.

Apostrophes

When we are speaking or writing, we often join two words together to make a shorter word. We make the word shorter by leaving out one or more letters from the original words.

When we write the shorter word down, we use an **apostrophe** (') in place of the missing letters.

Example: that is becomes **that's** (the letter **i** has been left out)

Top Tip

When we join two words together to make a new word, the shorter word is called a **contraction**.

 A   **Match the following contractions with the right words.**

she will	don't
do not	I'm
cannot	she'll
I am	can't

 B   **Rewrite the sentences below, adding the apostrophes in the correct places to the words in bold.**

1 Ruby **wasnt** wearing her reading glasses.

2 Betty and Clarice said **theyd** read all of the Ruby Redfort books.

3 Clarice **didnt** think the author had answered all her questions.

Writing a formal letter
Model writing

Read the formal letter below from Maria to her head teacher.

Class 3
Hill View School
School Road
Pine Valley

14 June 2013

Dear Mr Lopez,

I am writing to ask if Class 3 can have a party on the last day of term. Our test scores were the best the school has ever had, and we think we deserve a reward for being such good students!

We would like it if the party could be after morning lessons. Everything has been organized.

- All the tables and chairs will be cleared away.
- Every student will bring in one food/drink item, such as fruit or orange juice.
- There will be dancing and games. We will organize the music, too.

We look forward to hearing from you, sir.

Yours sincerely,

Maria

Guided writing

Notice how the sender of the letter does the following:

- Writes their address and the date at the top right-hand side of the page.

- Begins the letter 'Dear Mr Lopez'. This is the 'salutation'.

- Misses a line before the first paragraph.

- In the first paragraph, explains the purpose of the letter.

- Uses bullet points in the second paragraph to help make the arrangements clear.

- In the third paragraph, asks for a reply.

- Ends the letter with 'Yours sincerely' and writes their own name on a new line.

Glossary

bullet point
an item or idea presented in a list after a symbol such as a small circle

formal
official or businesslike

Top Tip

In a formal letter, when you know the name of the person you are writing to, you would sign off 'Yours sincerely'. If you don't know the name you would end the letter 'Yours faithfully'.

Writing a formal letter
Your writing

Imagine you are the head teacher. Write a letter in reply to Maria.

1 Write 'Dear Maria' in the first line.

2 In paragraph 1, state the purpose of your letter. Explain that Class 3 have been well behaved and deserve a party.

3 In paragraph 2, say you want Maria and the class to think about some possible problems with:

   • moving the tables and chairs (who will help move heavy tables?)

   • the party food

   • games, activities and music.

4 In paragraph 3, ask Maria to write back and let you know how Class 3 are going to make sure everything is organized properly.

5 Sign off the letter 'Yours sincerely'.

6 Write 'Mr Lopez' on the last line.

Formal letter checklist

To help you write your letter, use the checklist below. Then ask another student to double-check.

	Checked by me	Checked by another student
Start the letter with a salutation such as 'Dear Maria'		✓
Miss a line before starting the first paragraph	✓	
In paragraph 1, explain the purpose of the letter and agree that the class deserves a party		
In paragraph 2, ask Maria to think about the possible problems		
In paragraph 3, ask Maria to let you know how the problems will be managed	✓	
End the letter with 'Yours sincerely'		
On a new line write 'Mr Lopez'		
Choose good vocabulary		
Use capital letters and full stops correctly		
Use correct spelling		

6 Sharing cultures

"Aim for the highest cloud, so that if you miss it, you will hit a lofty mountain."

Maori proverb

Students greet each other with a 'hongi' at a school in New Zealand.

Let's Talk

1 Look at this picture of Maori people from New Zealand. What do you think is happening?

2 Maori people touch noses to greet each other. How do people in your country greet each other?

Look at the words in the Word Cloud and match them to the meanings here.

1 The first people to settle in New Zealand.

2 The way of life of a group of people, including their language, customs, art and music.

3 To meet or welcome.

Word Cloud

culture
greet
Maori

 Copy the sentences and use the following words below to fill the gaps.

**paint carving ceremonies
visitors dances**

The Maori hold special _____ to welcome _____ to their country. They often perform _____ and sometimes _____ their faces. Arts such as weaving and _____ are also important in Maori culture.

 The Maori people often perform dances to welcome visitors to their country. Work with a partner and discuss how being greeted in this way would make you feel. Explain your answer.

Play scripts from different cultures

This play script comes from a musical play based on a well-known Maori legend. According to the legend, the days were once too short. People could not finish their daily tasks and children had very little time to play.

Word Cloud
authority
hunting
mistakes
rush

Maui Catches the Sun

Child 1   *(practising stick games)* Oh, it's happened again! The sun's gone down and we can't see what we are doing!

Child 2   I keep dropping my sticks! We can't
5   practise in the dark!…

Woman 1   *(weaving)* It's always the same. Rush, rush, rush to get anything done before the sun goes down!

Woman 2   *(weaving)* We can't keep up with our work.
10   I'm only half way through weaving this mat *(holding up unfinished mat)* and now I can't see to finish it. I keep making mistakes!…

	Woman 3	We'll have to eat in darkness again!
15	**Woman 4**	That's right. We can't even see our food!…
	Child 3	*(to friend)* At least I can leave my vegetables and my mum won't know!…
20	**Woman 3**	*(standing up, moving off stage)* Come on everyone. Let's go.

(Bring the lights down to signal the end of the day.)

(Bring the lights back up to signal a new day.)

	Man 1	What can we do? Something must
25		be done to make our days longer. We cannot live like this…
	Village elder	*(stepping forward and speaking with authority)* Perhaps Maui can help us. Where is he?
30	**Man 2**	He's in the forest hunting. I'll go and find him. *(He exits.)*

From *Maui Catches the Sun* by Janet Grierson

Glossary

elder
an important older person in a community

signal
to give advance information about something

stage
the area where actors perform

Comprehension

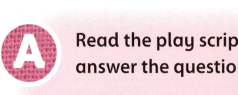

Read the play script on pages 88–89 and answer the questions.

1 What are the characters in the play complaining about? Find a sentence that tells you.

2 What are the children playing with?

3 Where does Man 2 say he is going to look for Maui?

4 What kind of food does Child 3 dislike?

B **What do you think?**

Use phrases from the play script to help with your answers.

1 Why does Woman 2 keep making mistakes in her weaving?

2 How does the actor playing Woman 3 know when to leave the stage?

3 How are the theatre lights used to show the end of the day?

4 The village elder speaks 'with authority'. What do you think this means?

C **What about you?**

Have you ever acted in a play, or would you like to? Talk about your answer with a partner.

Discussion time
Do you think it is important to learn about stories and customs from other cultures? Explain your answer to a partner.

91

Play scripts from different cultures (continued)

Maui Catches the Sun

Village elder (*slowly and thoughtfully*) If anyone can come up with an idea, Maui can. He has achieved many great things that have seemed impossible.

5

(*Maui enters.*)

Village elder (*calling Maui over to him*) Ah, Maui. Can you help us?…What can we do to lengthen our days? They are too short and the nights are too long. It's so frustrating for all of us.

10

Maui You are right. It's frustrating for me too. Just last night I was out fishing in the canoe. I had a big bite, I started to haul it in and it was a whopper! (*He shows exaggerated size with arm movements.*) I was just taking it off the hook when the sun went down…

15

20 **Narrator** Maui called his brothers together and told them of his plan. They would travel to the edge of the world to catch the sun in a snare made from flax ropes.

From *Maui Catches the Sun* by Janet Grierson

Word Cloud

canoe
exaggerated
frustrating
haul
snare
whopper

Comprehension

 A Which three sentences below are true?

1 The village elder thinks Maui is wise.

2 Maui wishes the days were longer.

3 Maui was fishing from the shore.

4 Maui decides to travel to the edge of the world.

 **Glossary**

flax
a plant from which linen is made

narrator
a person who comments on the action of a play

 B ## What do you think?

Use words or phrases from the story to help.

1 Why does the village elder think that Maui will be able to help?

2 Maui says he had 'a big bite' when he was fishing. What do you think this means?

3 Do you think the fish that Maui nearly caught was as big as he showed with his arms? Explain your answer.

 C ## What about you?

How do you think the legend ends? Do you think Maui and his brothers managed to make the days longer? Discuss your answer with a partner.

Irregular verbs

Top Tip

Remember: A verb in the **present tense** tells us what is happening **now**. Verbs in the **past tense** tell us what happened in the **past**. Many verbs in the past tense end with **ed.**

Some verbs are **irregular**. The means they do not follow the usual pattern when we use them in different tenses. One of the most common irregular verbs is the verb **to be**.

Present tense	Past tense
I am	I was
You are	You were
He is	He was
She is	She was
We are	We were
They are	They were

A Rewrite the following sentences, choosing the correct verb to fill the gaps.

1 The village elder _____ an important man. (are, is, were)

2 Maui _____ in the forest. (am, was, were)

3 Maori carvings _____ often made from wood. (are, was, is)

B Rewrite the following sentences in the past tense.

1 I am on my way to see a play.

2 The actors are ready to begin.

3 The play is based on a Maori legend.

Alphabetical ordering

A dictionary lists words in **alphabetical order**. Words beginning with **a** come first, followed by words beginning with **b**. Words beginning with **z** come last.

Many words start with the letter **a**, so we also need to look at the second letter.

Example:
agree comes before **arrive** in a dictionary because **g** comes before **r** in the alphabet.

 A Rewrite the words in alphabetical order.

1 tiger lion monkey zebra fish

2 yellow blue orange green pink

3 apple melon banana lemon peach

 B Look at these groups of words. For each group, write the word that would come first in a dictionary.

1 friend feel fish football

2 alligator adventure animal art

3 plant pencil paint present

 C Look up these words in a dictionary. Which comes first and why?

tonight today tomorrow

Writing a poem
Model writing

In the play script on pages 88–89 and 92, the Maori people want the sun to shine for longer each day. This poem describes what happens when the wind does not blow strongly enough.

Dear Mr Wind

Dear Mr Wind,

Could you please blow much harder

As we cannot

Sail our boats,

Dry our clothes,

Fly our kites!

Dear Mr Wind,

Could you please blow much harder

As we have

No breeze cooling us gently on a hot day

No waves crashing hard on the beach

No aeroplanes flying high in the sky!

Dear Mr Wind,

Please BLOW and BLOW
and BLOW and BLOW!

Moira Brown

Your writing

Write a poem that asks the sun to shine for longer. Use the same number of verses as the 'Dear Mr Wind' poem. The first four lines of the first two verses have been done for you.

Look at the notebook below and use the following ideas to help you write your poem:

- Write two more lines for the first verse shown below. Start each line with a verb.

- Then write two more lines for the second verse. Start each line with the word 'No'.

- Put an exclamation mark at the end of each verse.

How should you write verse 3?

Dear Mr Sun,
Could you please shine for much longer
As we cannot
Grow our vegetables,
....
....

Dear Mr Sun,
Could you please shine for much longer
As we have
No gentle warmth heating our cold land
....
....

Revise and check 2

Vocabulary

1 Copy the sentences below. Replace the words in bold with a word with a similar meaning from the following list.

noise giggle large honest teacher little

  a The **instructor** told the children not to **laugh**.

  b The **big** drum made a very loud **sound**.

  c My **small** brother was always **truthful**.

Punctuation

1 Rewrite the following sentences, adding the missing punctuation (capital letters, speech marks, commas, full-stops, exclamation marks and question marks).

  a you need to put a stamp on that letter the man told her

  b are you sure you have the right address she enquired

  c the boy chased the van shouting stop I have an important letter

  d oh no we've missed the post yelled the boy

2 Copy these sentences, writing the words in bold in full.

  a **They're** going to the aquarium on Sunday.

  b They **couldn't** wait to see their friends.

  c **We'll** pick you up at 4 o'clock.

Grammar

1 Rewrite the sentences with the correct verbs.

   a I __ getting ready to meet my friends. (is, am)

   b Ravi __ my favourite cousin. (are, is)

   c There ____ a basket of clothes by the river. (was, were)

Spelling

1 Copy the table below and complete with singular or plural nouns.

Singular	Plural
beach	
	glasses
	fields
watch	
box	
	dishes

2 Write these words in alphabetical order.

   care warm pain slow price colour power

3 Add the suffix –*ly* to the following words, using the correct spelling.

   happy quiet easy loud

It's a mystery!

"Most people – and that includes you and me – know that things that belong to other people belong to other people."

Alexander McCall Smith

Let's Talk

1 What do you think is happening in this picture?

2 Do you think adventure and mystery stories are more exciting than other kinds of stories?

Mysterious words

 A Read the words in the Word Cloud and match them to the meanings below.

1 Something that nobody understands.

2 An unusual and exciting experience.

3 A person who tries to solve a crime.

Word Cloud

adventure
detective
mystery

 B Copy the sentences below and use the correct words to fill the gaps.

fingerprints   magnifying   footprints

The burglar left muddy _footprints_ on the floor and _fingerprint_ on the wall. The detective used a _magnifying_ glass to look for clues.

 **C** Would you be a good detective? With a partner, think of three clues that would help you solve a crime. Explain your answer.

Adventure and mystery stories

This story takes place in Botswana, Africa. It is about a young girl named Precious Ramotswe, who wants to be a detective. Precious and her friend Tapiwa are walking home from school. Tapiwa tells Precious about a mystery at school.

Word Cloud

crumbs
stolen
thief

Stolen Cake

"There must be a thief at school," said Tapiwa, looking over her shoulder in case anybody heard what she had to say.

5 "I brought a piece of cake to school with me this morning. I left it in my bag in the corridor outside the classroom." She paused before she went on. "I was <u>really</u> looking forward to eating it at break-time."

…"Somebody took my cake," Tapiwa
10 complained. "I had <u>wrapped</u> it in a small piece of paper. Well, it was gone, and I found the paper lying on the floor."

Precious frowned. "Gone?"

"Eaten up," said Tapiwa. "There
15 were crumbs on the floor and little bits of icing. I picked them up and tasted them. I could tell that they came from my cake."

"Did you tell the teacher?" asked Precious.

20   Her friend sighed. "Yes," she said. "But I don't think she believed me. She said, 'Are you sure you didn't forget that you ate it?' She said that this sometimes happened. People ate a piece of cake and then forgot that they had
25   done so."

Precious gazed at Tapiwa. Was she the sort of person to eat a piece of cake and then forget all about it? She did not think so.

"It was stolen," said Tapiwa. "That's what
30   happened. There's a thief in the school. Who do you think it is?"

"I don't know," said Precious. She found it hard to imagine any member of their class doing something like that. Everybody
35   seemed so honest.

From *Precious and the Monkeys: Precious Ramotswe's Very First Case* by Alexander McCall Smith

Glossary

honest
truthful

icing
a sweet covering on cakes

sighed
breathed out heavily to express sadness

103

Comprehension

 Read the story on pages 102–103 and answer the questions.

1 Find the phrase in the story that tells us where Tapiwa left her cake.

2 What three clues did Tapiwa find that told her that her cake had gone?

3 What did the teacher think had happened to Tapiwa's cake?

4 Find the word that describes what Precious thought of her classmates?

What do you think?

Use phrases from the story to help with your answers.

1 How do you think Tapiwa felt when her teacher did not believe her?

2 Does Precious think that Tapiwa has a good memory? Explain your answer.

3 Find three strong verbs in the story. (Remember, you looked at strong verbs in Unit 1, page 18.) Why do you think the author chose to use these verbs?

Discussion time

Do you think Tapiwa would have forgotten if she had eaten the cake herself? Was the teacher right not to believe her? What do you think the teacher should have said? Give your reasons.

What about you?

How would you feel if somebody stole your snack at school? What would you do?

Adventure and mystery stories (continued)

When Tapiwa's cake goes missing, Precious decides to find the thief. She bakes a cake and leaves it next to some glue on a shelf outside the classroom.

Trick Cake

It happened suddenly. One moment everything was quiet, and the next there came a great squealing sound from outside. The squealing became louder and was soon a sort
5 of howling sound, rather like the siren of a fire engine.

…"What on earth is going on?" asked the teacher. "Open the door, Sepo, and see what's happening."

10 …What was happening was that two monkeys were dancing up and down alongside the shelf, their hands stuck firmly in the mixture of glue and cake. Struggle as they might to free themselves…they were thoroughly and
15 completely stuck to the cake.

"See," shouted Precious in triumph.

"There are the thieves, Mma. See there!"

From *Precious and the Monkeys: Precious Ramotswe's Very First Case* by Alexander McCall Smith

Glossary

Mma
a word used in Botswana to show respect to an older lady or your teacher

siren
a loud warning sound

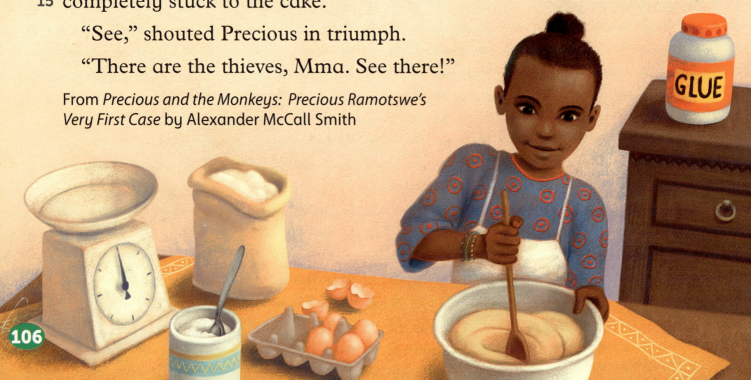

Comprehension

 A **Which three sentences below are true?**

1 The monkeys' hands were stuck to the glue. ✓

2 The monkeys escaped with the trick cake.

3 Precious tricked the monkeys. ✓

4 Precious solved the mystery. ✓

 B **What do you think?**

Use phrases from the story to help with your answers.

1 Why did Precious put glue on the shelf? *So she can trap the monkeys.*

2 Why did the monkeys start to squeal? *Because they were trapped.*

3 What does the author say the monkeys sounded like? *Like a siron.*

4 Was Precious pleased that her idea worked? Explain your answer. *Yes, because she finally figured out who ate her cake.*

 C **What about you?**

Do you think Precious was right to do what she did? Give reasons for your answer.

Challenge

Do you think Precious will grow up to be a good detective? Work with a partner and describe what you know about her character.

107

Prefixes, non- and mis-

A **prefix** is a group of letters added to the beginning of a word. When you add a prefix to a word, you change the meaning of the word.

 A The prefix *non-* means 'not' or 'opposite of'. Rewrite the following sentences, adding the prefix *non-* to fill the gaps.

1 The detective thought what the burglar said was _non_ sense.

2 The author wrote _non_-fiction books.

3 We booked a _non_-stop flight from London to Cairo.

 B The prefix *mis-* means 'wrong' or 'false'.

1 Rewrite the following words, adding the prefix *mis-*. take → mistake

behave judge take lead

behave → misbehave
judge → misjudge
lead → mislead

2 How does the prefix change the meaning of the words? It does the opposite of the words.

3 Write a sentence using each of the words you made in 1. He got in trouble from the teacher because he mis-behaved!

Prefixes, anti-, co- and ex-

Prefix	Meaning	Example
anti-	against	antifreeze
co-	joint, together	coordinate
ex-	out of, away from	export

 A **Match the following words to the meanings below.**

exhale   anticlockwise   coexist

1 In the opposite direction to the way the hands of a clock move round.

2 To breathe out.

3 To live together or at the same time.

 B **Copy the following sentences and fill the gaps with the words below, adding the prefix *anti-, co-* or *ex-*.**

1 "A monkey has eaten my cake!" ex claimed Tapiwa.

2 The detective co operated with the policeman.

3 The nurse gave the patient an anti biotic to make him feel better.

 C **Look up the meaning of the following words in a dictionary. Then make up three sentences of your own, using each of the words.**

explode   antidote   coincidence

Pronouns

A **pronoun** is a word that we use instead of a noun.

Examples:

Precious made the cake and **she** put **it** on the shelf.

We use the pronoun **she** instead of the name 'Precious' and the pronoun **it** instead of 'the cake'.

Pronouns

I	me
we	us
he	him
she	her
they	them
you	it

A Copy the following sentences and replace the words in bold with pronouns.

1 Precious made a trick cake and used **the trick cake** to solve the mystery.

2 Precious asked Tapiwa if **Tapiwa** had spoken to the teacher.

B Copy the sentences and fill the gaps with one of the pronouns below.

we I you

1 "Did _____ eat the cake yourself?" asked the teacher.

2 "_____ both want to find out what happened," Precious said to Tapiwa.

3 "_____ am pleased that my plan worked," said Precious.

More pronouns

Some pronouns are singular and some pronouns are plural.
Singular pronouns: I, he, she, me, him, her, it, you
Plural pronouns: we, they, them, us, you

When we use a singular pronoun with a verb, we use a singular verb. When we use a plural pronoun with a verb, we use a plural verb.
Examples:
I was at school.
We were at home.

 Rewrite the following sentences changing the pronouns in bold from singular to plural.

1 The detective showed **me** the muddy footprints.

2 **I** used a magnifying glass to look at the clues.

3 **She** hoped **he** could solve the mystery.

 Copy the following sentences and choose the correct verb to fill the gaps.

1 They _____ surprised to hear the monkeys squealing. (were, was)

2 She _____ to put glue on the shelf. (decides, decide)

3 He _____ the classroom door. (open, opens)

Writing an adventure story
Model writing

Read the story below about Stefania and Ivan's adventure in a forest.

> ### Glossary
> **quivered**
> trembled
> **retorted**
> replied

The Adventure in the Forest

"It's your fault!" shouted Ivan, his small, round face red and angry.

"No," retorted Stefania, stamping her feet, "it's yours. You asked mother if we could play in the forest, and now we're lost and…" Her voice quivered, "no one is ever going to find us!"

Fearfully, they both looked around. The hundreds and hundreds of tall trees blocked out the light from the sky so that there was not a path to be seen, anywhere.

"What was that?" whispered Stefania.

"What?"

"That noise. Can't you hear it?"

"No, don't be silly…"

But at that point Ivan stopped. There was a noise. And it was the loudest noise he had ever heard. A roar, in fact – and whoever (or whatever) was making it, it seemed to be coming towards them. ROAR…!

Guided writing

Notice that the story includes:

- Characters – the people in the story
- A setting – where the story happens
- A problem – something that is wrong

Notice how the writer builds up the excitement and sense of danger in three stages:

- The children are lost.
- They cannot see any paths.
- There is a loud noise.

The children feel scared. The reader wants to read on to find out how the children get out of the woods and back to their mother and everyday life. The children are going to have to be very brave – and clever!

Notice that the writer uses dialogue to keep the plot moving along and a new paragraph when there is a change of speaker or subject.

Writing an adventure story

Your writing

Now finish the adventure story about Stefania and Ivan. Remember to keep the story exciting to make your readers want to read more. Here are some ideas to help you:

Characters	*Describe how your characters react to what happens to them. Use adjectives to describe what they look like and what kind of personalities they have. It is also important to make sure the reader knows how the characters are feeling.*
Setting	*When you describe the setting, remember to use all the senses – what can your characters see, hear, smell, taste and see? Is the setting safe or is it dangerous?*
Dialogue	*Instead of just describing what is happening, use conversation between your characters to keep the story moving along.*

Writing plan

Use this paragraph plan to help you finish the story.
You can use the ideas here, or your own.

1 Stefania and Ivan discover what made the roaring noise

What made the roaring noise in the forest? Was it a fierce animal or a monster? Or was it something else? You decide.

2 Stefania and Ivan escape

How did Stefania and Ivan escape from the forest and find their way back home?

3 Stefania and Ivan arrive home safely

What happened when they arrived at home? How did Stefania and Ivan feel?

Glossary

personality the qualities that make up a person's character

react to act in response to something

Top Tip

When you are writing your story, remember to use **powerful adjectives** and **action verbs** to make your writing exciting. Adjectives such as 'fierce', 'terrifying' and 'brave', and verbs such as 'hurried', 'screamed' and 'grabbed' will make your story come to life.

8 Our world

A friend who is far away is sometimes much nearer than one who is at hand.

Kahlil Gibran

Let's Talk

1 The boy in this picture lives in the Arctic region of northern Alaska. What do you think it is like to live there? How do you know this from looking at the picture?

2 Would you like to live there? How is it different from your country?

Look at the words in the Word Cloud and match them to the meanings here.

1 Very far away and isolated.

2 Very cold.

3 The regions around the North Pole.

Word Cloud

Arctic
frozen
remote

 Read about Michael, who is describing where he lives. Copy the sentences and use the words to fill the gaps.

warm   neighbours   summers   region

I live on a farm in a remote _____ of Australia. We live hundreds of kilometres from our nearest _____. It is _____ all year round here and the _____ are hot and dry.

 Find out more about Alaska and Australia on the Internet. Work with a partner and talk about how the countries are similar to your own country and how they are different.

Non-chronological reports

Here is some more information about Michael. It is not a story (fiction). It is true (non-fiction).

Michael

A sheep and cattle station in the South Australian outback is home to Michael, his sister and their parents. Because he lives so far from a school, Michael does his
5 schoolwork alone and talks to his teacher over a two-way radio.

Animals

As well as cattle and sheep, there are other animals on the station. The family keep *chooks*,
10 (chickens) for their eggs and ducks for their meat. There are dogs and also horses used for *mustering* (rounding up) the cattle.

Word Cloud

ranch
sheared
two-way radio
windmills

"I help feed and water the dogs, chooks, ducks, horses and cattle. When I grow up I would like my own cattle station so I could be like Dad."

Australia

Australia's population is small in relation to its size. Some farming families live hundreds of kilometres from their neighbours.

Australia

Outdoors

Michael spends a lot of time outdoors. He loves
15 taking the dogs for a run and riding his bike
around the station. Twice a year he goes to
camp where he meets other children his age.

Sheep

There are 1,200 sheep and 550 cattle on the
20 ranch. Once a year, the sheep are sheared for
their wool. Even Michael and Rebecca [his
sister] get involved, although most of the work
is done by hired sheep hands.

*"The best thing about living in the outback are the
windmills, the open spaces and sunsets. The worst
thing is not being able to see my friends."*

Toys and games

25 Michael plays on his own with his toys – trucks,
tractors and a motorbike. He loves reading
Outback Magazine, and he also watches
television and plays games on his computer.

From *A Life Like Mine: How children live around
the world*, Dorling Kindersley

Glossary

outback
a remote region of
Australia

**sheep and cattle
station**
a large farm that
raises sheep and
cattle

sheep hands
farm workers who
look after sheep

*"I talk to my friend,
Naish, on the school
radio after lessons. He
lives on Bulgunnia
Station, 630 km (390
miles) from here."*

Comprehension

 Read the text on pages 118–119 and answer the questions.

1 Name four kinds of animals that are raised on the farm.

2 Where does Michael do his schoolwork?

3 What three things does Michael like most about living in the outback?

4 What are the dogs and horses used for on the farm?

What do you think?

Use phrases from the text to help with your answers.

1 Why do you think it is difficult for Michael to see his friends?

2 Find four subheadings in the text. Why do you think these are included?

3 Do you think Michael is helpful on the farm? Explain your answer.

4 Find the three examples of quotes (words spoken by Michael). How do these help you understand more about Michael's life?

Discussion time

Discuss with a friend three reasons why you think it is important for children who live on farms in the outback to meet at camp twice a year?

C What about you?

How would you feel if you lived on a remote farm and had to do your schoolwork at home? Discuss your answer with a partner.

121

Non-chronological reports (continued)

Desert Meerkats

Where they live

Meerkats are desert animals that live in groups
called gangs. Meerkats dig underground
burrows. The burrows are safe places where
they give birth to their young. They sleep in
5 their burrows at night. In the daytime they
leave their burrows and set off in search of food.
When meerkats are in danger, they run to their
burrows to keep safe.

What they eat.

Meerkats eat worms, grasshoppers, lizards,
10 snakes, scorpions, eggs and fruit. Most of all
they love grubs!

How they protect each other

When it's really hot, they have a nap. One
meerkat stays awake and looks out for danger.

From *Going Underground* (Project X) by John Malam

Word Cloud

burrows
grubs
underground

Africa

Meerkats live in the
Kalahari Desert, which
is in Africa.

Africa

Kalahari
Desert

A **Which two sentences below are false?**

1 Meerkats look for food at night.

2 This text is non-fiction. ✓

3 Meerkats only eat plants.

4 Meerkats like to eat grubs. ✓

Challenge

The Kalahari Desert is home to many kinds of animals, including giraffes and lions. Find out about other animals that live in the Kalahari Desert. You can use a book or the Internet.

B **What do you think?**

Use phrases from the text to help with your answers.

1 Why do you think meerkats build underground burrows? To go in when there is danger.

2 The report about meerkats is separated into three paragraphs. Think of two subheadings, one for the second paragraph and one for the third paragraph. 1 paragraph where th

3 Why does one meerkat stay awake when the others have a sleep during the day? To look out for danger.

C **What about you?**

Give three reasons why you think meerkats are interesting animals.

Irregular verbs

Verbs in the **past tense** often end with the letters **ed**. Some verbs are **irregular**. This means they do not follow the usual pattern.

Two common irregular verbs are **to have** and **to go**. In the past tense, 'have' changes to **had** and 'go' changes to **went**.

Examples:
I **have** fun when I **go** to camp.
I **had** fun when I **went** to camp.

 A Copy these sentences. Underline the verbs and write whether they are in the present or past tense.

1 Australia has a small population for its size.

2 Michael had a friend called Naish.

3 The children went to camp twice a year.

 B Rewrite these sentences in the past tense.

1 The giraffe has a very long neck.

2 At the end of the day, the meerkats go into their burrows.

3 The lioness has two young cubs.

Compound words

Compound words are made when two words are joined together to form a new word.

Examples:
bed + **room** = bedroom
lady + **bird** = ladybird

A Match the words on the left with words on the right to make compound words.

grass
foot
straw

→

ball
berry
hopper

B Copy these sentences and use the words below to make compound words to fill the gaps.

hedge   birth   bow

1 Sunita made a cake for the _____ day party.

2 The _____ hog is covered in spines.

3 We saw a beautiful rain_____ in the sky this morning.

> **Challenge**
> Re-read the reports on pages 118–119 and 122 and find four examples of compound words. Write a sentence for each word you find.

C Write a sentence for each of the compound words you made in A.

Clauses and connectives

Sentences are made up of one or more **clauses**. A **simple** sentence is just one clause that makes sense on its own.
Examples: Meerkats sleep in burrows. They look for food during the day.

Some sentences are made up of two simple clauses joined together. These are called **compound** sentences.
Example: Meerkats sleep in burrows and they look for food during the day.

We join clauses together in a sentence using **connectives**.
Examples: **and**, **but**, **so**

Top Tip

A **clause** is a group of words that includes a **verb**. If a group of words does not contain a verb, it is called a **phrase**.

A Copy these compound sentences adding a connective to fill the gaps.

1 Meerkats love to eat insects _and_ they also eat lizards and snakes.

2 It was very hot _So_ the meerkats had a nap.

B Join the sentences together with a connective to make a compound sentence.

1 Michael has a two-way radio. He uses it to talk to his friends. _and_

2 Michael lives a long way from school. He does his schoolwork at home. _So_

Clauses and commas

Some sentences include clauses that would not make sense on their own. These are called **complex sentences**.
Example: **Although I left early**, I was late for school.

The clause 'Although I left early' does not make sense on its own. It is called a **subordinate clause**.

When a subordinate clause comes first in a sentence, it is followed by a **comma** (**,**) to separate it from the rest of the sentence.

 A Copy these sentences and underline the subordinate clauses.

1 When I got home from school, I was hungry.
2 After I had eaten my breakfast, I cleaned my teeth.

 B Copy these sentences adding a comma in the correct place.

1 Before I left the house, I picked up my school bag.
2 While it is in its burrow, the meerkat is safe.

 C Look at the text on page 122. Find an example of a comma used between a subordinate clause and the rest of the sentence.

Writing a non-chronological report
Model writing

Lions

How big are lions?
Lions are the second largest cat species in the world. The average male lion weighs around 180 kg (400 lb) while the average female lion weighs around 130 kg (290 lb).

Where do lions live?
Lions mostly live in the grasslands, savanna and open woodlands of Africa, but they also live in the Gir Forest in India.

Do lions live on their own?
No, lions live in groups called prides. Sometimes, a pride can contain as many as 40 lions, but they can also have as few as three!

What do lions eat?
Lions are carnivorous animals, which means they eat meat. The animals they eat include deer, zebras, giraffes and hippos. Believe it or not, the female lions are the hunters. However, it is the male who will eat first, then the females and the cubs last.

Glossary

cub
a young lion

savanna
a grassy plain in a hot country with few trees

Guided writing

A report has to make information clear and straightforward so that the reader can understand it. Notice examples of the following features in the report about lions.

Feature	Example
Subheadings are questions and make it clear what the paragraph is about	*Where do lions live?*
Explanations of new words	*Lions are carnivorous animals, which means they eat meat.*
Paragraphs begin with a topic sentence, telling us what the paragraph is about	*Lions mostly live in the grasslands...*
Use of the present tense	*The average male weighs...*
Use of connectives between sentences to link ideas	*However, it is the male...*

Top Tip

Using connective words such as 'However' and 'Sometimes' at the beginning of sentences helps to link ideas together. Varying your sentence openings, with phrases such as 'In the morning' and 'As soon as', will also make your writing more interesting.

Writing a non-chronological report

Your writing

Write a factual report on an animal of your choice. You will probably need to do some research first, perhaps on the Internet or by looking in a book.

Once you have done your research, start to plan your report. Make your report four or five paragraphs long. Decide on the subheadings for each paragraph and list the key facts you plan to include under each subheading.

Plan your writing using a chart like this:

How big are lions?	*Second largest type of cat.* *Details of the weight of a male and female.*
Where do lions live?	*Details of where they live in Africa and India.*
Do lions live on their own?	*Live in prides. Size of prides.*
What do lions eat?	*Carnivores. Examples of what they eat.* *Females are hunters. Males eat first.*

Top Tip

You can find lots of information books in a library. Non-fiction books are grouped together on the shelves by subject. To find out if a book contains the information you are looking for, look at the contents page at the front of the book or the index at the back.

Report checklist

Copy out a chart like the one below to help you write a good report!
Check your work as you go along and put ticks on your chart.

	Yes	No	Sometimes
Report has a title	✔		
Each paragraph has a subheading, making it clear what the paragraph is about	✔		
First sentence of each paragraph is a topic sentence, which introduces the main subject of the paragraph			
Present tense is used			
Difficult new words are explained	✔		
Connectives are used between sentences			
Varied sentence openings are used	✔		

9 Why do we laugh?

"The most wasted of all days is one without laughter."
E. E. Cummings

Let's Talk

1 Look at these three pictures. Do you think they are funny? Why?

2 What makes *you* laugh? Do you tell jokes or play tricks on people?

Funny words

 A Look at the words in the Word Cloud and match them to the meanings here.

1 A noise which we make when we think something is funny.

2 Another word for funny.

3 A short, funny poem with five lines.

4 A short, funny story.

Word Cloud

amusing

joke

laugh

limerick

 B Read aloud the following limerick. Copy the lines below and use the following words to fill the gaps.

fat day cat sat hay

There once was a pony so _____

He couldn't stand up so he _____

He tried walking one ____

Fell down flat in the _____

And he nearly squashed the _____ .

 C Read the limerick in B with a partner and make a list of the words that rhyme. Think of three more words that rhyme with cat and day.

133

Poetry

This poem by Kit Wright is a narrative
poem – a poem that tells a story.

Dad and the Cat and the Tree

Word
Cloud

climber
ladder
slipped
wobbly

This morning a cat got
Stuck in our tree.
Dad said, "Right, just
Leave it to me."

5 The tree was wobbly,
The tree was tall.
Mum said, "For goodness'
Sake don't fall!"

"Fall?" scoffed Dad,
10 "A climber like me?
Child's play, this is!
You wait and see."

He got out the ladder
From the garden shed.
15 It slipped. He landed
In the flower bed.

134

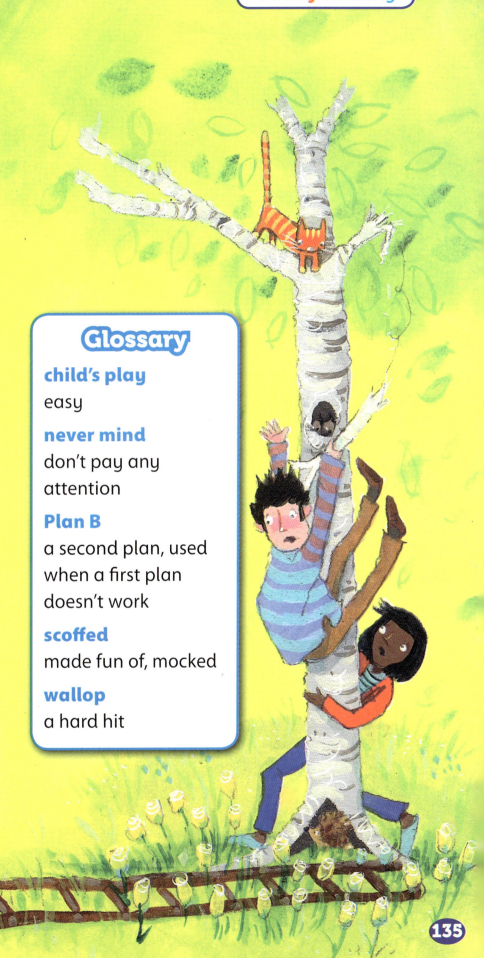

"Never mind," said Dad,
Brushing the dirt
Off his hair and his face
20 And his trousers and shirt,

"We'll try Plan B. Stand
Out of the way!"
Mum said, "Don't fall
Again, OK?"

25 "Fall again?" said Dad.
"Funny joke!"
Then he swung himself up
On a branch. It broke.

Dad landed *wallop*
30 Back on the deck.
Mum said, "Stop it,
You'll break your neck!"

"Rubbish!" said Dad.
"Now we'll try Plan C.
35 Easy as winking
To a climber like me!"

(continues on page 138)

Glossary

child's play
easy

never mind
don't pay any
attention

Plan B
a second plan, used
when a first plan
doesn't work

scoffed
made fun of, mocked

wallop
a hard hit

Comprehension

 A **Read the poem on pages 134–135 and answer the questions.**

1 Find two adjectives that describe the tree.

2 What two expressions does the poet use to tell us that Dad thought climbing the tree was easy?

3 How do we know that Dad had more than one plan?

4 Which two sentences in the poem tell us where Dad landed?

What do you think?

Use phrases from the poem to help with your answers.

1 Why do you think the poet sometimes uses exclamation marks in the poem?

2 What do you think Mum thinks about Dad climbing the tree?

3 Which verbs and adjectives do you think are most effective in the poem so far? Explain why you like them.

4 Which words and phrases in the poem do you find most funny?

 What about you?

Think about something funny that has happened to you. Tell a friend your funny story.

Discussion time

Do you think this poem is funny? Why? With your class, make a list of the kinds of things that can make a poem funny.

Poetry (continued)

Dad and the Cat and the Tree (Part 2)

Then he climbed up high
On the garden wall.
Guess what?
He *didn't fall!*

5 He gave a great leap
And he landed flat
In the crook of the tree-trunk –
Right on the cat!

The cat gave a yell
10 And sprang to the ground,
Pleased as punch to be
Safe and sound.

So it's smiling and smirking,
Smug as can be,
15 But poor old Dad's
Still

Stuck
Up
The
20 Tree!

Kit Wright

Word Cloud

smirking
smug

Glossary

crook
where a branch
meets a tree trunk

pleased as punch
very pleased

safe and sound
free from danger
or harm

Comprehension

 Which three sentences below are true?

1 Dad climbed onto the garden wall.

2 Dad rescued the cat.

3 The cat landed safely on the ground.

4 Dad got stuck in the tree.

 What do you think?

Use phrases from the poem to help with your answers.

1 Which verse in the poem do you find most funny? Give reasons for your answer.

2 What phrases tell us how the cat feels at the end of the poem?

3 Towards the end of the poem, the poet describes the cat as 'smiling', 'smirking' and 'smug'. Why do you think he chose those words?

4 What does the poet do to make the ending seem more dramatic?

 What about you?

What do you like best about this poem? What surprised you at the end of the poem?

Using a dictionary and thesaurus

A **dictionary** is a list of words arranged in alphabetical order. If you look up a word in a dictionary, you will be able to find out what it means. This is the word's **definition**. Most dictionaries will also tell you what kind of word it is, such as noun, adjective or verb.

If you look up a word in a **thesaurus**, you will find a list of other words with similar meanings.

Top Tip

Using a **thesaurus** can help you avoid repeating the same word (such as 'said') over and over again in your writing. This will make your writing more interesting.

 A Look up the words in bold in a dictionary. Write out the meaning and say whether the word is a noun, adjective or verb.

1 The tree was **wobbly**.

2 The **ladder** slipped.

3 The cat **smirked**.

 B Use a thesaurus to find two words that you could use instead of the words in bold.

1 The cat felt **happy** to be safe.

2 We read the poem and it made us **laugh**.

3 We thought it was **funny** when Dad got stuck in the tree.

Homonyms

A **homonym** is a word that sounds the same as another word and often has the same spelling, but with different meaning.

Examples:
This dog has a loud **bark**!
The tree trunk is covered in **bark**.

Top Tip

Homonyms are often used in jokes to make a 'play on words'. In the following example, there is a play on the word 'bark'.

Why did the cat jump down from the tree?

Because it saw the tree bark.

A **Match the homonyms below to their meanings.**

watch train wave

1 The high, moving part of water in the sea /To move your hand to say hello or goodbye.

2 A small clock worn on the wrist/To look at something carefully.

3 To practise hard for something/Railway carriages pulled by an engine.

Challenge
Work with a partner and use a dictionary to find two other examples of words that are spelled the same but have different meanings. Write a sentence for each of the meanings.

B **Copy the following sentences and put a circle around the homonyms.**

1 The boy found his blue top in the top drawer.

2 The post box was next to the fence post.

3 The ruler used a ruler to draw straight lines.

Writing a limerick

Model writing

Read aloud the limerick below.

Limerick

There was an Old Man with a beard,
Who said, "It is just as I feared!
Two Owls and A Hen,
Four Larks and a Wren,
Have all built their nests in my beard!"

Edward Lear

Guided writing

Notice the words that rhyme in the limerick. Can you see a pattern?

When you write a limerick, remember the following rules.

- Limericks have five lines.

- Lines 1, 2, and 5 rhyme with each other. Line 4 rhymes with line 3. This is called an AABBA rhyming pattern.

- Lines 1, 2 and 5 have seven to ten syllables.

- Lines 3 and 4 have five to seven syllables.

Your writing

Use the ideas below to help you write your own limerick.

Top Tip

When writing a limerick, it helps to say the words out loud and tap out the rhythm.

Example

1 Choose the name of a boy or girl and use it at the end of the first line.

There was a young boy named Guy

2 Make a list of words that rhyme with the name.

shy, pie, why, try, fly, sky, cry, spy

3 Write line 2, using one of the rhyming words from the list.

Who ate such a very big pie

4 Write lines 3 and 4 to continue the story.

*It made him explode
All over the road*

5 Write the last line to complete the story – end with another rhyming word from your list.

And even into the sky!

When you have finished your limerick, ask a friend to check it:

• Does the poem have five lines?

• Does it have an AABBA rhyming pattern?

• How many syllables does each line have?

• Is it funny?

Does your friend have any tips for how you could make the limerick better?

Revise and check 3

Vocabulary

1 Copy the sentences below, filling the gaps with the correct word.

   a The Arctic is a _____ place. (remote, amusing)

   b The ladder was _____. (smug, wobbly)

   c Precious wanted to solve the _____. (adventure, mystery)

2 Write two sentences for each of the following homonyms.
Use a different meaning of the word in each sentence.

   bark wave ruler

3 Choose one word from the top row and one word from the bottom row to make four compound words. (Remember, compound words are made when two words are joined together to make a new word.)

   tooth lady rain sun
   flower bow bird brush

Punctuation

1 Copy the following sentences, adding commas in the correct places.

   a Lions eat zebras giraffes hippos and deer.

   b After he had found the muddy footprints the detective solved the crime.

   c Once it had landed safely on the ground the cat felt smug.

   d Because he lives a long way from school Michael does his schoolwork at home.

144

Grammar

1 Copy these sentences, filling the gaps with the correct pronouns.

a Karl's dad said he would take _____ to play basketball. (him, he)

b Karl asked _____ and Rahim if we wanted to go, too. (me, I)

c Karl said _____ would pick us up at 3 o'clock. (they, them)

d After the game, Karl's dad took _____ home. (we, us)

2 Rewrite the following sentences, underlining the subordinate clause.

a Although female lions are the hunters, the males eat first.

b Dad decided to climb the tree because the cat was stuck.

c When they heard a loud noise, the children were scared.

d Tapiwa talked to her teacher after her cake went missing.

Spelling

1 Match the prefixes to the correct word and write a sentence for each word.

| mis |
| non- |
| anti |
| co |
| ex |

| clockwise |
| behave |
| operate |
| stop |
| claim |

Yasmin's Parcels

Chapter 1

Yasmin nibbled at the piece of bread in her hand. She was eating slowly, trying to make it last. She knew there was no more food in the house. She looked at the rest
5 of her family. They were all so pale and thin. Mama and Papa and six little brothers and sisters were all squashed into the two dark rooms of their home. Papa was lying on the bed. Mama was
10 rocking the baby in her arms.

"If only Papa's back would get better," sighed Mama. "Then he could find a job."

"And we wouldn't all be so hungry,"
15 said Yasmin.

She finished her bread.

"I wonder how your Grandmama is," said Mama.

"I think I'll go round and see her,"
20 said Yasmin.

It was very hot outside, but Yasmin hurried along the dusty streets. Soon she reached the tiny old cottage and pushed open the door.

25 "Hello, Grandmama," she called. "How are you today?"

"Very well, thank you."

Grandmama's voice sounded croaky and weak and Yasmin noticed how old and ill she

30 looked. Grandmama was hungry, too.

I wish I had something to give her, thought Yasmin.

After a little while, Yasmin went home. She sat in the corner, thinking. What could she do

35 to help? Suddenly, she had an idea.

"I'm the oldest child in the family," she said to herself. "My family is starving. I must go and find some food."

She jumped up and ran to the door.

40 "I'm going out," she said.

"Don't be long," said Papa.

"No, Papa."

"Keep away from strangers," said Mama.

"Yes, Mama," called Yasmin as she went out

45 into the street.

147

Yasmin walked into the town. First, she searched through rubbish bins, but she found nothing to eat there. So she went to the market place. She let her fingers trail through the
50 beautiful fluttery silk scarves that rich people bought. She saw pottery jugs, colourful clothes, reed baskets, leather sandals and woven cloths, but she didn't find any food.

Suddenly, she stopped. There in front of her
55 was a small door that she had never noticed before. The door was ajar so she peeped inside.

"Come in," called an old crackly voice. It made Yasmin jump. She remembered what Mama had told her and she stepped back.

60   "Who are you?" she called.

Chapter 2

Yasmin heard slow shuffling feet then the door opened wide. An old man stood in the doorway.

"I'm just an old man who makes pottery jugs," he said to Yasmin. "What do you want?"

65   "My family is very poor," said Yasmin. "I'm looking for some food."

"I haven't enough for myself," said the old man, sadly. "I can't help you, but I would be very grateful if you would do something 70 for me."

Yasmin looked at the old man. She couldn't help feeling sorry for him.

"What do you want me to do?" she asked with a smile.

75   "My kiln has gone out," said the old man. "So I can't fire my beautiful jugs. Will you find me some wood so I can light it again?"

Yasmin was glad to help the old man. She ran along the road and gathered some sticks 80 from under the trees. When her arms were full she carried them back to him.

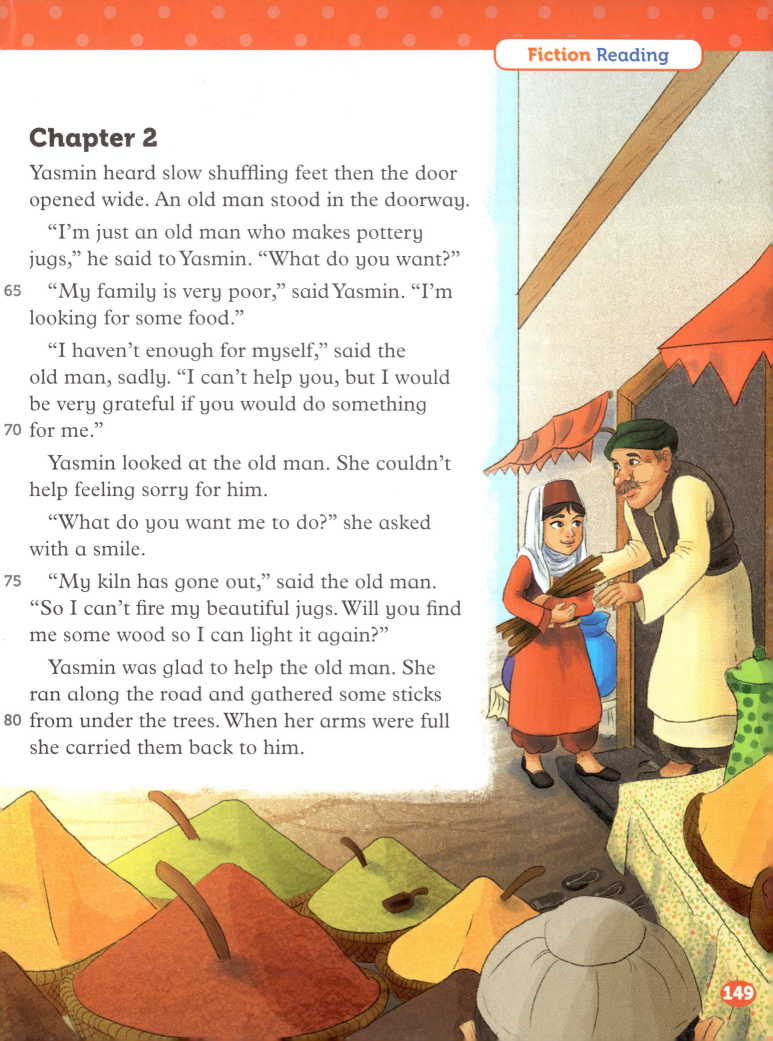

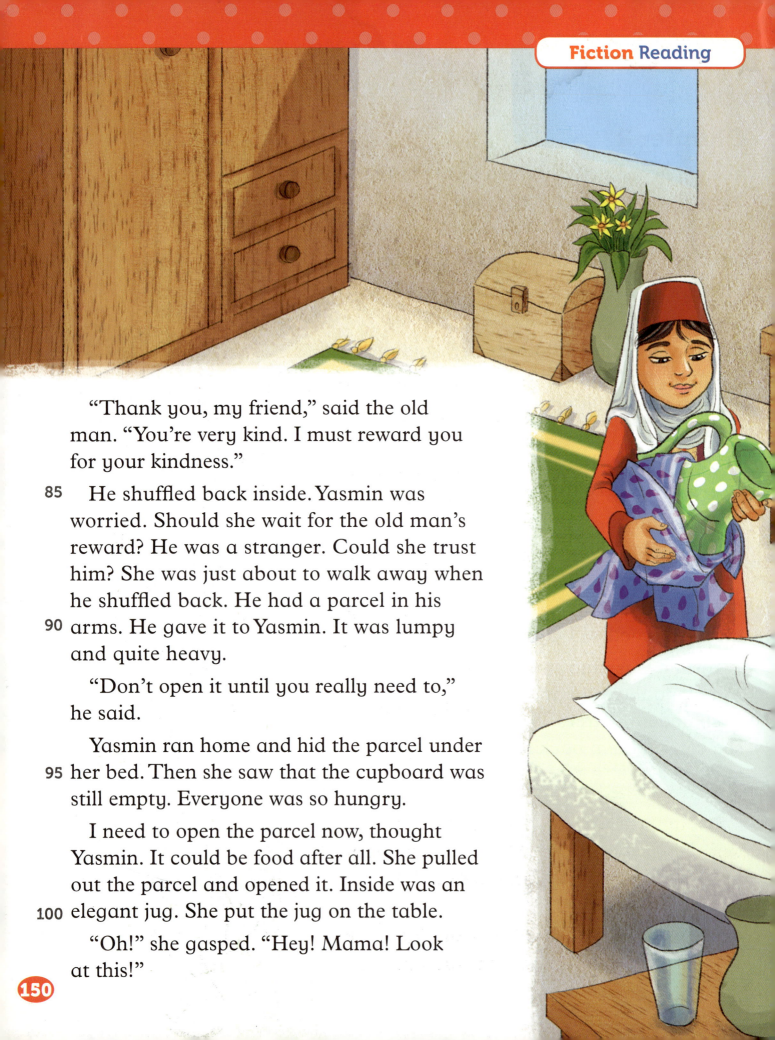

"Thank you, my friend," said the old man. "You're very kind. I must reward you for your kindness."

85 He shuffled back inside. Yasmin was worried. Should she wait for the old man's reward? He was a stranger. Could she trust him? She was just about to walk away when he shuffled back. He had a parcel in his
90 arms. He gave it to Yasmin. It was lumpy and quite heavy.

"Don't open it until you really need to," he said.

Yasmin ran home and hid the parcel under
95 her bed. Then she saw that the cupboard was still empty. Everyone was so hungry.

I need to open the parcel now, thought Yasmin. It could be food after all. She pulled out the parcel and opened it. Inside was an
100 elegant jug. She put the jug on the table.

"Oh!" she gasped. "Hey! Mama! Look at this!"

The jug was full of milk.

"Where did you get this?" asked Mama.

05 "An old man gave it to me," said Yasmin, "because I helped him."

Yasmin shared out the milk and put the jug down on the table. Then she picked up her cup and sipped. It tasted so good! She drank it all 10 down in one go and licked her lips. She felt so much better already.

But what a surprise! The jug was full again.

"It's magic," she whispered as she poured some more.

15 Each time she put the empty jug on the table it filled up.

"It's never going to run out," said Yasmin. "I'll take some to Grandmama in the morning."

But in the middle of the night, Yasmin was 20 woken by a sound. Smash! She leapt out of bed just as a cat disappeared out of the kitchen window.

"Oh, no!" Yasmin cried. The jug lay on the stone floor, broken into a thousand pieces.

Chapter 3

125 Tears trickled down her face as she swept up the pieces.

"What happened?" asked Mama.

"A cat must have knocked it down," cried Yasmin. "And now there's nothing left for
130 Grandmama."

Sadly, Yasmin went back to bed.

In the morning, she looked at her family. Their eyes seemed so big in their thin faces.

"Everyone is still hungry," Yasmin sighed.
135 "I'll have to search for food, again." She jumped up and ran to the door.

"I'm going out," she said.

"Don't be long," said Papa.

"No, Papa."

140 "Keep away from strangers," said Mama.

"Yes, Mama," called Yasmin as she went out into the street.

This time, Yasmin ran along by the river.

She searched in the reeds and the mud of the
45 riverbank, but there was no food to be found.
She was slowly making her way home when she
met an old woman, sitting on the ground with a
reed basket in her hands.

"What are you doing?" Yasmin asked.

50 "Making baskets," said the old woman.
"What do you want?"

"My family is starving," said Yasmin. "Have
you got any food you could spare us?"

"I have hardly enough for myself," said the
55 old woman. "I can't help you, but perhaps you
could do something for me?"

The old woman looked very sad. She
reminded Yasmin of Grandmama.

"What would you like me to do?" she asked
60 with a smile.

"I have run out of reeds," said the old
woman. "I can't finish making my baskets. Will
you find some reeds for me?"

Yasmin ran back along by the river. She
65 collected some reeds and carried them to the
old woman.

"Thank you, my friend," said the old woman. "You're very kind. I must reward you for your kindness."

170 She reached behind her and pulled out a parcel. She handed it to Yasmin.

"Don't open it until you really need to," said the old woman.

Yasmin ran home and hid the parcel
175 under her bed, but it was no good. Everyone was starving.

She fetched the parcel and opened it. Inside was a strong reed basket. Yasmin put it on the table.

180 "Oh!" she gasped. "Mama! Quick!"

The basket was full of bread.

"Where did you get this?" asked Mama.

"An old woman gave it to me," said Yasmin, "because I helped her."

85   Everyone took a piece of bread. It was the best Yasmin had ever tasted. Her brothers and sisters were smiling. They loved it, too.

    Yasmin looked at the basket on the table. But what a surprise! It was full again.

90   "I'll take some to Grandmama in the morning," said Yasmin as she ate her second piece of bread.

    But that night, Yasmin woke in time to see someone climbing out of the window. She saw

95 that the basket had gone.

    "Thief!" she cried. "Mama! Papa! The basket has been stolen! Now there's nothing left for Grandmama."

Chapter 4

In the morning, Yasmin's little brothers and
200 sisters were crying. They were still hungry.
Yasmin knew she had to go out again.

"They need my help," she sighed.

She jumped up and ran to the door.

"I'm going out," she said.

205 "Don't be long," said Papa.

"No, Papa."

"Keep away from strangers," said Mama.

"Yes, Mama," called Yasmin as she went out
into the street.

210 Yasmin jogged through the fields to the edge
of the mountains. But the fields were dry and
dusty and the mountains were hard and rocky.
She soon realized she would not find anything
to eat there.

215 She was just about to return home and
was walking past a big cave in the side of a
mountain when she heard someone crying. She
looked into the cave and saw a little boy sitting
by a big loom. He looked just like her brother.

220 "Why are you crying?" she asked.

"I must finish weaving this tablecloth," said the boy. "Or I will be in big trouble."

"So why don't you just finish it?" asked Yasmin.

25 "I've run out of thread," said the boy and he began to cry again.

"Don't cry," said Yasmin kindly. "I'll see if I can find you some more thread."

She dashed out of the cave and back across 30 the fields. Soon she found some animal hair caught on a bush. She gathered handfuls of the hair and hurried back to the boy.

"But I can't weave that!" cried the boy. "I need a long thread."

35 There was a spinning wheel in the corner.

"I'll spin it for you," Yasmin said.

When she had spun the thread, she gave it to the boy.

"But I can't use that!" cried the boy. "It's the 40 wrong colour."

Yasmin sighed, but she ran out into the fields again. She found some berries and carried them back to the cave. Then she squashed the berries and dyed the thread 245 with the juice.

When the boy saw the bright thread, he smiled.

"Thank you, my friend," he said. "You've 250 saved me from an angry master. I must reward you for your kindness."

He reached under the loom and picked up a parcel. He gave it to Yasmin. It was square and very light.

255 "Don't open this until you really need to," he said.

"Thank you," said Yasmin and she ran home, but she didn't hide the parcel this time.

Chapter 5

Yasmin opened the parcel. Inside was a
60 tablecloth just like the one the boy had been
making. She spread it over the table. Suddenly,
the table was covered with fantastic things to
eat. She stared at the meatballs and rice, the
stuffed vine leaves and the peppers, the water
65 melon and peaches, the apricots and cherries.

"Come and look at this!" she called.

Mama and all her little brothers and sisters
ran to the table. Even Papa got up and stared.

"Where did you get this tablecloth?"
70 Mama asked.

"A little boy gave it to me," said Yasmin,
"because I helped him."

"You're such a kind girl," said Mama, giving
Yasmin a hug. "Thank you."

75 "Can we eat? Can we eat?" chanted
the little brothers and sisters.

Yasmin held up her hand.

"Not yet," she said. "Wait. We can't eat a
mouthful until our guest arrives."

280   She left the house and dashed to Grandmama's cottage.

"Quick, Grandmama," she said. "Come with me. I have a surprise!"

Everything was delicious! Mama, Papa, 285 Yasmin, Grandmama and all the little brothers and sisters ate and ate.

But what a surprise! As soon as they had eaten the last mouthful, the table was full again.

That night Yasmin hid the tablecloth under 290 her pillow.

"We must look after this tablecloth for ever," she said.

From that day Yasmin's family were never hungry again. And, most important of all, 295 Yasmin always made sure that there was plenty left for Grandmama!

Yasmin's Parcels by Jill Atkins

Word Cloud

ajar
elegant
kiln
loom
nibble
trickle

160